# GETTING THE WORD OUT
How Managers Can Create
Value with Communications

# GETTING THE WORD OUT

## How Managers Can Create Value with Communications

*Frank M. Corrado*

**BUSINESS ONE IRWIN**
Homewood, Illinois 60430

Sponsoring editor: Cynthia A. Zigmund
Project editor: Karen J. Nelson
Production manager: Irene H. Sotiroff
Designer: Larry J. Cope
Art coordinator: Mark Malloy
Compositor: Precision Typographers
Typeface: 11/13 Times Roman
Printer: Book Press, Inc.

### Library of Congress Cataloging-in-Publication Data

Corrado, Frank M.
    Getting the word out : how managers create value with
communications / by Frank M. Corrado
        p.    cm.
    ISBN 1-55623-785-5
    1. Communications in management—United States.  2. Public
relations—United States—Corporations.  I. Title.
HD59.C728   1993
    658.4'5——dc20                                                                   92-23730

*Printed in the United States of America*
1  2  3  4  5  6  7  8  9  0  BP  9  8  7  6  5  4  3  2

For my parents,
Anne and Mike, with
deep gratitude and respect

# PREFACE

Writing a book in the last decade of a century can be scary. Any prognosis you consider giving seems to take on more weight. This is certainly true when trying to deal with a subject like communication, and especially when the technology of communication is in such bewildering flux.

The specific focus of this book is the management of communication inside U.S. organizations and how managers can utilize its enormous power in creating value and moving the organization forward.

In *Media for Managers*, the predecessor to this volume, I tried to make the point, as former Gulf Oil Chairman James Lee summed up in the Foreword to that book, that corporate communications, like war, is too important to be left entirely to the communications professionals. My thesis was that business was being evaluated more and more by the U.S. public as having an important societal role, and that it must communicate to a diverse number of constituencies on broader issues such as rights, environment, and consumer protection. I argued that business managers urgently needed to develop communications skills and apply them both inside and outside the organization.

Now, a decade later, the major business schools are seriously introducing training to provide managers with basic communication skills. A need for strategic communication skills is just now becoming apparent. In *Media for Managers*, I also tried to underscore the importance of media training, crisis communications, and better financial communications. The need for all three became painfully apparent in the 1980s.

Media and crisis communications training has become imperative for management throughout the United States. As a matter of fact, the training courses I conduct around the country often involve managers far down into the organization, who are now expected to be able to talk, when necessary, with a television crew, a newspaper reporter, or even an angry crowd.

*Getting the Word Out* attempts not only to provide the manager with a broad overview of the communications function in corporate America in the 1990s, but also to educate him and her on how communication can create value and drive the organization forward, to make money and also to fulfill a responsible role as a primary institution in United States society.

One of the most rewarding outcomes of the rethinking of the corporation has been the new interest in mission/vision/values. While some CEOs have just gone through the exercise because they feel it's *au courrant*, an equal number or more have embraced this effort because they understand how important it is to have a clear direction to be going. Also, they understand that leadership is more important than management.

In researching material for this book, I realized that the new frontier for communication efforts is *inside* the organization. There has been so much restructuring in U.S. business and so much bad press aimed at senior management in the last few years that before launching sophisticated external communications programs, the first step for U.S. business management is a quiet soul-searching. From that exercise hopefully will result some consistently credible messages to communicate to employees and finally external audiences.

For all our damnation of the Japanese, in the end, they do seem to care more about employees and to communicate better with them. And they are very successful. And so, quite a bit of this book is devoted to the subject of communicating better with employees.

*Getting the Word Out* also encourages utilizing communications more in the marketing effort. The numbers are beginning to clearly show that good marketing P.R. is currently more credible and effective than advertising.

*Getting the Word Out* is divided into three general sections. The first looks at the changes that have taken place in the U.S. corporation from a communication perspective, especially regarding senior management, line management, employees, and the role for professional communicators on staff. We strongly believe that the CEO should carry the further designation of "Communications Director." This title would only recognize what *de facto* is already the case.

The second section describes how communication is assuming a major marketing role and how companies need to appeal to the new "green" consumer. The third section provides a perspective on managing external issues that impact the organization's ability to operate in society. Finally, we include, in some appendixes, communication approaches for the public and the nonprofit sector, and finally some assistance for evaluating and measuring the value that communication creates. Hopefully this will help answer the questions, Can you prove communication works? Can you prove it adds value?

We will also cover some particularly difficult issues such as crisis communications, environmental and community issues, the risk-averse citizen, and television, which our society needs to learn to get better control of.

While lunching one day with some former colleagues at Northwestern's Medill School of Journalism, I confirmed my experience that computers have really made writing more difficult because we seem to write more tentatively. Certainly, I can see the change and yet, like other writers, I ask, How did we ever do it before, with just a typewriter? Writing a book takes more than machines, and I enthusiastically want to give credit where credit is due.

Thanks to many people: my editor at BusinessOne Irwin, Cindy Zigmund, and her assistants in Chicago for their confidence and help; my colleagues at Communications for Management, Inc. International in Chicago; my partner and cheerful friend Edward Stecki who introduced me to the world of data bases; my colleague and copyreader, Lindsey Gorney, and my good-spirited helpers Karen Harley and Jim Gavitt. I am especially indebted to Robert Nadeau of our staff who did so much in the way of focusing attention on the concept of value creation. My longtime colleagues Jim Horton of James Arnold & Associates and Dick Hyde of Hill & Knowlton were helpful at different times, as was Bob Irvine and marketing researcher Joe Boscarino. Susan Heitsch of First Chicago has often provided me with a valuable perspective on communications professionals. I also want to thank Lauren Barnett and her staff at the American Society for Health Care Marketing and Public Relations for giving me the opportunity over the last six years to meet and work with hundreds of wonderful communicators around the country through ASHCMPR seminars. And I certainly owe much gratitude to my clients around the country who have provided me with the opportunity to see what's going on.

Finally, I want to thank my family: my parents, Mike and Anne Corrado; and my brother Paul; my good wife Karen, who kept the house running while I danced with the keys; and my children—Kelli, Mike, and Joe, who are themselves each worth a book and more.

Frank M. Corrado

# CONTENTS

*PREFACE*                                                    vii

Chapter   1
A MILLION MESSAGES A DAY                                      1

*Chapter   2*
THE CEO AS COMMUNICATIONS DIRECTOR                            9

*Chapter   3*
MANAGING COMMUNICATIONS                                      26

*Chapter   4*
COMMUNICATING WITH EMPLOYEES                                 39

*Chapter   5*
HUMAN RESOURCES COMMUNICATION                                64

*Chapter   6*
COMMUNICATING TO THE MARKETPLACE                             83

*Chapter   7*
THE GREEN MANAGER                                            97

*Chapter   8*
COMMUNICATING WITH EXTERNAL
AUDIENCES                                                   117

*Chapter   9*
MEETING THE PRESS                                           133

*Chapter 10*
CRISIS COMMUNICATIONS                          156

*APPENDIXES*
A. GOVERNMENT AND THE NONPROFIT
   COMMUNICATION                               177
B. MEASURING COMMUNICATIONS VALUE    191

# Chapter One

# A Million Messages a Day

We have more communication than we know what to do with. The technology of this age overwhelms us. The cereal package we open each morning carries an average of 1,268 words. The morning paper contains an average of 125,000 words. Business produces over 72 *billion* photocopies annually—in this, the age of the paperless office.[1] It takes 1.5 Boeing 747's to carry that aircraft's technical documentation. The Cable News Network provides visual images to hundreds of millions of people in over 100 countries on a real-time basis via satellite. At least 74 other full time cable TV networks are available on a national basis. When you have finished reading this book, you will have digested another hundred thousand words or so.

A lot of communication is just filling the channel. The voracious appetite of constant, real-time media today buries any one particular message. Henry David Thoreau made a very prescient observation in *Walden* on the introduction of the telegraph: "We are in great haste to construct a magnetic telegraph from Maine to Texas; but Maine and Texas, it may be, have nothing important to communicate."[2]

A major problem today with news and public affairs is that in covering them, television (TV) in particular, turns them into entertainments.[3] This certainly has been a reason for the enormous success over the years of "60 Minutes"—the entertainment value in seeing the good guys ride out to corral the bad guys and shooting bullets at their feet to make them dance. And "60 Minutes" is one of the best shows of its kind.

No crisis today is so great that we can't break for a commercial. To watch the Democratic candidates during the early local debates in 1992 being bullied by news anchors to get on to the next topic because time was awasting, underscored how truly trivialized the media makes any event, regardless of its importance. Encouraged by the successes of independent candidate Ross Perot in by-passing the newsmedia and launching his campaign via the Larry King Live show on CNN, 1992 candidates flocked to the talk show *en masse* to deliver their messages live and in real time to a call-in audience, thus outflanking the sound-bite syndrome of the 6 o'clock news.

Whether it's entertainment or news presented as entertainment, watching television, studies show, beats almost everything else, including sex and eating out, as America's most enjoyed form of recreation. Watching TV is the dominant leisure activity of the U.S. public—accounting for 40 percent of free time. Watching TV has resulted in an average drop in sleeping time of 15 minutes per night.[4]

Television is at the popularity apex of a marvelous technology bazaar. Consider that over half the homes in the United States have *cable television*. As of 1992, 7 out of 10 homes had a video cassette recorder *VCR*. The year 1993 will mark only the first decade that *personal computers* have generally been in widespread use. Also, in 1992, Motorola was moving ahead on a series of 75 low-orbit satellites that would allow use of a cellular telephone *anywhere on earth* before the start of the 21st century. And in 1992, AT&T announced introduction of a new two-way *videophone* via standard telephone wire. Just prior to that, AT&T announced it was offering a new form of data transmission, frame relay, which would move information at 1.5 megabytes per second.[5]

Predictions are that 98 percent of all media in the United States will be digital by the turn of the century as computers, communications, consumers, and information reach towards total interactivity. The challenge of telecommunications is to make the "pipes" big enough to push all the signals through.

The net effect is creation of new partnerships between cable, data, computer, and video companies to provide consumers with the maximum ability at home and work to interact one-on-one with the outside world. The messages will become more targeted, as information suppliers use new technologies to provide information on demand to consumers in multimedia formats.

Major events, thanks to Ted Turner's CNN, have become available almost anywhere in the world. Certainly, before long, learned studies will be forthcoming on the impact of this worldwide communications system on the downfall of Communism. One reporter noted that communication in the Gulf War and the invasion of Panama had created an "instantaneous loop of information" in which CNN was getting better information about the enemy than the Joint Chiefs of Staff. Even the White House was getting its information from CNN, not the CIA. In response to a question from Jane Pauley, Senator John Warner of

Virginia said, "My source of information is your source." She commented, "What a scary thought that is, Senator."[6]

As the speed in our age increases, issues march across the public stage in rapid-fire order. Columnist Russell Baker notes how troubles of society tend to become boring to people. The television audience quickly tires of complex stories like the S&L crisis, prewar U.S. support of Iraq, and other nonvisual events. Commentators remember Andy Warhol's often quoted prediction that television would make everybody famous for 15 minutes. The missing caveat is that they better make those 15 minutes interesting and make sure their stories are conceptually easy.

Towards this brave new world, the U.S. business organization sails onward in the 1990s. Navigating the waters will not be easy, given today's major economic concerns, which include a need for strategies for doing business in the new world marketplace. For senior management, this means finding a new management approach that blends some of the best ideas from successful Japanese and European business models into an approach that makes sense in a U.S. culture. Some of the strategies in meeting these challenges will include an emphasis on better customer service, a greater commitment to producing quality products, and a new push for greater productivity inside the organization.

Business organizations must also deal with some very negative fallout from the 1980s, which may result in a new swing towards greater government regulation to control some of the excesses of that earlier era. These excesses caused great economic upheaval for workers and communities throughout the United States. Between 1984 and 1991, for example, AT&T eliminated over one hundred thousand jobs. Over 26,000 of those jobs were in manufacturing and 8,000 jobs were sent to plants outside the United States.[7]

Coming into the 1990s, the United States was reeling from a trillion dollar debt, a gigantic trade imbalance, a lack of perceived competitiveness and inventiveness on the part of industry, and a heedless depletion of natural resources.[8]

For business there is also the accelerating pace of information and communication. Markets seem to emerge and disappear overnight and product life cycles shrink. To adapt to the rapid changes, companies are trying to develop flexibility, nimbleness, and customer focus. The result is constant reorganization. A few companies really seem to be able to manage the dynamics of change—General Electric (GE), Xerox, and British Air are a few examples. Others like Compaq, Sears, Roebuck & Co.,

General Motors Corp. (GM), and International Business Machines Corp. (IBM) are companies that have not been able to react as quickly.

At GE, for example, chief executive officer (CEO) Jack Welch has become famous for cutting out layers of management, pushing decision making down lower into the organization, and getting workers more involved through monthly gripe sessions with their bosses. "The early 80s were a hardware decade," he told *USA Today*, "The 90s and late 80s are what we call software. We're working desperately to get everyone participating in the process."[9]

## NEW BUSINESS IMPERATIVES FOR COMMUNICATIONS

To cope in the new environment, business must reevaluate how it does many things, including communicate with its publics. Great communication should be like the U.S. telephone system—a transparent effort, with technology so good that when anything goes wrong, it is a major news story.

Great communication should hardly ever be noticed. An organization communicates seamlessly when employees continually and informally communicate up, down, and across the organization. Employees and managers tell the company's story to customers, shareholders, government, the community, and other audiences.

But, while many organizations may be doing a better job of getting the word out, their deeds sometimes contradict their words. A company that downsizes while increasing the CEO's compensation is not "walkin' like it's talkin'," to quote a catchphrase of the corporate excellence movement. A company that touts its environmental record and is then cited for pollution violations falls into the same category. The medium of successful communication is credibility. When the deeds don't match the words, self-correcting mechanisms step in in the forms of the grapevine, the government, or the media.

When the new communications environment of the 1990s is matched with the new corporate priorities, imperatives for communication emerge in four areas:

1. Employees—The remaining frontier in management is people. The science of business management has mastered the other factors of production—capital, resources, and technology—but the effective use of people remains a challenge. With the dissolution of the longstanding contract of

"loyalty for job security," a more strained relationship has developed between company and employee, just as management is embracing an emphasis on greater employee empowerment and involvement.

Our contention is that the role of communication will not be to try to mend any rift between employer and employee, but rather to create measurable value for the organization through its effective use in the organization. This means that management will find it increasingly important to improve communication with employees in words and deeds in order to meet its goals of greater productivity, customer service, and quality.

2. Customers—For a number of reasons, including diminishing credibility and overuse, advertising is being supplemented more often, and sometimes is being replaced, by increased use of public relations. As companies strive to break through the clutter of messages in the marketplace, they are finding that utilization of the news media—a communication channel that is perceived to have a higher credibility level—can more effectively deliver information to targeted customers.

3. Society—Customers are also citizens and consumers. More than ever, the old differentiations are disappearing. A company that wants a stronger market position today knows that "green marketing"—positioning itself as environmentally responsible—will have stronger appeal, since three fourths of U.S. citizens consider themselves environmentalists.

The management of public issues ranges from handling operational concerns such as product labeling and safety; to issues involved in worker relations, like health care and minimum wage; to larger issues like the opening of foreign markets.

4. Management—It is not easy to make generalizations about the impact of communication on management. Everyday we see situations in which companies with poor communication policies and values survive, and even prosper. Exxon, which was widely condemned for its awful communication in the 1989 Valdez incident, had its best year ever in 1991. Communication is not the *sine qua non* of business, but it has become more of a factor than ever before in today's message conscious and technology driven environment.

## CREATING VALUE WITH COMMUNICATION

For the above reasons, managers must begin to get a better grasp on improving communication with customers, employees, and society. Unfortunately, the business schools have not taught managers to think at a strategic level—beyond business issues. Managers are taught to ask questions such as What business should we be in that will give us a better rate of return? Managers today need to be able to ask the follow-up questions like, Should we get into a business that has so much environmental baggage? or How should we change management behaviors to get our employees to add value?

The schools that produce communicators have likewise failed to provide the kind of strategic training that gives a staff communicator the skills that add value and perspective to the organization. Instead, communicators arrive at the door knowing the mechanics of writing, video production, and publicity. However, many, if not most, can't answer strategic questions about how to change management behaviors or how to motivate employees to add value. Nor do these communicators know enough about evaluation and measurement to prove that what they do works.

As a result, management has been turning more and more to the human resource staff for help with employee communications, to the marketing department for help with marketing communications/public relations, and to the legal department for help in dealing with the media and other external audiences. As a result, many in the communications profession are working feverishly trying to demonstrate how communication can create measurable value.

Inside the organization, the old top-down authoritarian model is passing into the shadows. Business managers know they must become business leaders who can have a vision, set a mission, and establish strong values that get everybody heading in the same direction. Communications is now not a department, but a priority. Organizational communication focuses not only on transmitting information, but changing the behavior of employees so that they will do a better job of moving the organization towards achieving its goals.

One of the real success stories of communication has been in improving *marketing* and reducing advertising costs. Because of the voracious appetite of new media venues such as cable, there are more opportunities for delivering sales messages. What seems to be working exceptionally well is getting the news media to put its mantle of credibility over a sales pitch— whether it's marking the introduction of a new Crayola color, celebrating the Idaho potato or the birthday of peanut butter, or selling a new sports center complex for St. Louis.[10]

Regarding the organization's *external* environment, many are becoming aware that there will be an economic cost for companies that continue to fight a rear-guard action, and deliver messages that run against the grain of changed societal values—such as environmentalism, equality, and consumer protection.

Public interest groups, the media, and almost every segment of U.S. society are becoming more sophisticated and better informed. They know which political buttons to push and are not afraid to push them with the media, the courts, and the legislative process. The communication function of the organization creates value by monitoring and developing interventions to protect the company's position in society.

Public relations counselor Philip Lesly has noted that "management is increasingly oriented to measurable and computer-driven facts; to the visible and tangible rather than the nuances of human feelings and motivations." He foresees that the field of communications (or public relations) "will probably go on growing in numbers and in universality of use—while slipping in stature and influence."[11]

Lesly argues that communication creates the kind of value that is not easily measurable—like avoiding mistakes, helping management understand the "human climate," advising cooperation and networking rather than conflict, and developing positions and perceptions. "But that's lost sight of in the rush to deal only with what can be spelled out in numbers or column inches," he adds. "So the high-level functions are ignored."

If history is an accurate guide, U.S. business will soon enter an era of more restrictive government control as the pendulum swings back from the wide-open '80s, government's laissez-faire stance, and the resultant near bankruptcy of the U.S. economy.

Communication skills will be more important than ever before as the business executive seeks to defend the company's traditional role in society, while attempting to position the company in a brave new world of national industrial policy, international economic warfare, and calls for more domestic programs correcting educational and social failures of this most recent era.

A positive outcome of the 1980s has been a dramatic change in the way management views two of its key stakeholders—the *employee* and the *customer*. Commitment to quality, customer service, and employee empowerment have taken hold in both manufacturing and service industries, with very positive results.

## SUMMARY

The role of communication in rebuilding the company of the 1990s cannot be overstated. The greatest irony is that in the new world of communication technology that we have created, "high touch" has won out. The greatest successes come from the person-to-person, one-on-one communication: supervisor to employee, employee to employee, employee to customer—characteristic of the customer and quality initiatives. On a broader scale, this means that jobs previously designated for handling by a specific communications department are now becoming the responsibility of the entire management team.

And that's how we begin: naming those in the organization who have communication responsibilities, starting with the CEO, then the supervisor, the human resource manager, and finally the professional communicator. There's work for all. Each must work to accomplish the organization's mission. Each must deliver credible messages to the organization's key audiences and each must share in the successes and failures.

## ENDNOTES

1. Al Ries and Jack Trout, *Positioning: The Battle for Your Mind* (New York: McGraw-Hill, 1981), pp. 11–20.
2. Quoted in Neil Postman, *Amusing Ourselves to Death, Public Discourse in the Age of Show Business* (New York: Penguin Books, 1986), p. 65.
3. *Ibid*, p. 87.
4. John P. Robinson, "I Love My TV," *American Demographics*, September 1990, pp. 24–27.
5. "AT&T Plans to Offer Faster Data Transmission," *New York Times*, November 19, 1991, p. D–2.
6. James Warren, "Instant Reporters Born for TV," *Chicago Tribune*, December 21, 1989, p. 16.
7. Associated Press, "Labor Says Jobs the Issue at AT&T," *Chicago Tribune*, March 31, 1991, p. 3–3.
8. John B. Oakes, "Bush's Calumnies: A Dangerous Game," *New York Times*, November 11, 1988, p. 17.
9. Mindy Fetterman, "A Beacon for CEOs: CEO of Year Will Focus on Soft Stuff, *USA Today*, July 15, 1991, p. 01B.
10. Public Relations Society of America, "1991 Silver Anvil Winners, Index and Summaries," New York, 1991.
11. Philip Lesly, "Public Relations in the Turbulent New Human Climate," *Public Relations Review*, Spring 1991, pp. 1–8.

*Chapter Two*

# The CEO as Communications Director

## THE STATE OF SHIPS

The metaphor of business is sailing—a world of shipbuilders and sailors, captains and navigators, rough seas and safe ports. It is no great surprise that for the longest time the seas off Long Island Sound produced sailing's great aces. The two-fisted entrepreneurs, or the shipbuilders, who with bluff and daring and extraordinary energy followed their dreams and built their companies from the ground up, included Wannamaker and Field, Vanderbilt and Ford, Watson and Taylor, and McCormick and Deere.

In time, these builders of the great ships of business were replaced by more temperate sea captains—managers—who kept to the bridge and guided the ships through calm waters. But when the rough seas of late 20th-century foreign competition began to swell, and complacent crews became unsure of themselves and the ship's course, the winds forced change.

A new kind of captain was needed—one who could not only pilot the ship, but also make it move faster through storms, forge a tighter-knit crew, and lead in battle.

## LEADERSHIP

Back in the "Leave It to Beaver" days of U.S. life, when U.S. business had only a domestic market to worry about, management was a premier skill. Today, in the face of withering international competition for world markets, high debt, lower-quality products, overstaffed managements, and lower-skilled workers, there is a great need for the skills of *leadership*. One writer summed it up succinctly: "Most American corporations today are overmanaged and underled.''[1] Leadership helps companies get through change. As in the military, you can manage soldiers in peacetime but in war, you have to lead them. As Peters and Waterman wrote in their book *In Search of Excellence*, the leader needs to get people roughly headed together in the same direction. The emphasis is on setting a vision, raising emotions, and emphasizing values that will lead to success.

Leaders don't create budgets or long-term plans. They set a direction. "We want to build the highest-quality widget for the experienced widget user," clearly lays out a vision, a commitment to produce a product at a certain quality level for a specific market segment. The real question here is whether the company's stakeholders—employees, customers, investors, suppliers, and others—buy into that vision, and whether that vision is an achievable one.

The major challenge for the CEO, or leader, is *selling* this idea to the stakeholders, with the emphasis on lots of communication. Managing the implementation of this vision requires communication, but not near as much as *selling* the vision. Leadership today is defining a new problem, not solving an old one. Bringing about change requires not only selling a vision, but increasing the organization's energy level. Just like a ship needs to crank up the engines or trim the sails when it makes a turn, an organization needs a burst of energy when it tries to change.

Motivating employees to change requires action as well as communication. It's like the old saw, "Are you walkin' like you're talkin'?" A company that touts change and then continues to reward employees based on longevity, instead of performance, is not well led. The real communication to employees is that "the CEO's just blowing smoke." People begin to believe when they see that performance really *is* rewarded. Too many companies, however, rush headlong into restructuring just to pump up the numbers and to get rid of older, more expensive employees. Or management puts up "quality" banners and goes back to business as usual.

What makes people want to follow a leader has a lot to do with the amount of *credibility* they attach to that leader—the leader's integrity, the believability of the message, the leader's track record, and the energy the leader brings with it. The credibility of top corporate managers is at an all-time low in the 1990s. One reason for this is that CEOs are asking employees for sacrifices but are not cutting back their own salaries or perquisites (perks). Hay Group attitude studies since the late 1980s have shown growing negative feelings by middle managers.[2] Lou Harris polling has shown that managers do not necessarily want more money. Instead, they want more recognition for their contributions, honest communication, and ethical management.

The most visible gap is the pay gap—with some CEOs getting one hundred times as much, or more, than some of their workers. Basic respect for individual workers appears to be missing. An exception to this situation is Southwest Airlines. It is often cited for excellent employee-management relations and it has the most productive employees of any airline. One consultant believes the reason for this is that employees believe the company isn't "trying to milk them in order to swell the bottom line."[3]

Increasing criticism of high CEO salaries, new pressures from large pension fund investors, and a new activism by usually docile corporate boards has put new pressures on CEOs. For example, Lee Iacocca of Chrysler was told to set a retirement date; Robert Stempel of GM was removed as head of the board's executive committee; Andrew Signal of Champion International was pressured to cut executive pay at a time when investors could have done better with Treasury bills than with Champion's stock. The real issue, experts said, was generally a lack of executive accountability in companies. It appears that investors were starting to exercise their ownership.[4] The gods were beginning to appear mortal. To top it all off, in June of 1992, the Securities and Exchange Commission proposed changes that would, for the first time, require companies to present the specific factors on which executive pay is based and to describe how this package is related to the company's performance. The efforts of the leader will also be successful to the extent that employees feel empowered to take action in the name of a common vision. Management's job is to help with implementation, with the systems, and with the organizing that will make the plans work.

Another characteristic of today's business environment includes speed of change. Leadership that overrides the more deliberate and necessarily slow management process is necessary for fast change. Leadership must extend beyond senior management, down into the organization to the level of the individual supervisor, or first-level manager. Research has shown that this skill is transferable through the organization as long as it is clearly described, encouraged, and tested.

The medium for managing change in U.S. business is communication. But only recently have top corporate leaders begun to understand that communication can directly impact the bottom line—for better or for worse. At least one study shows that almost four out of five CEOs *do* believe that their communications efforts can really have that impact.[5]

## CEOs AND COMMUNICATION

There are many reasons why the CEO has been slow to embrace the importance of communication:

1. CEOs have not perceived that communication was important to their success. Former DuPont chairman Irving Shapiro was once quoted as saying that in the early days of the 20th century "you could get by in business by following four rules: stick to business, stay out of trouble, join the right clubs, and don't talk to reporters."[6] Once upon a time, that may have been possible. Today, everybody is watching.

For a stark contrast in CEOs, communication style consider James Burke, the head of Johnson & Johnson (J&J) and Lawrence Rawls, CEO of Exxon Corporation. Burke became a legend in corporate *leadership* for having saved the Tylenol brand after a series of poisonings scared U.S. consumers in 1982. Rawls, on the other hand, has become a symbol for poor *management* because of Exxon's missteps in handling the Exxon Valdez disaster just seven years later.

Tylenol went on to regain its market share. However, Exxon not only suffered a dollar loss—the clean-up cost of over $3 billion—but the U.S. petroleum industry was slowed in its attempt to open up the Arctic National Wildlife Refuge for oil development. Analysts said that J&J's marketing savvy in being able to gauge and react to public opinion, as well as its strong customer-focused culture, made the difference. The lessons for senior management from earlier crises such as Tylenol, Bhopal, and the NASA Challenger tragedies were missed by the very inwardly focused Exxon.

2. Communications has been wrongly perceived as a cost that does not produce a measurable return. Another reason communications has been neglected as a top management priority over the years is that communications' impact on the bottom line has not been apparent. Communications researchers have had a very difficult time establishing linkage between how well a company communicates and its profitability.

Strangely enough, evaluation and measurement tools that have proven effective in advertising are rarely brought to bear on organizational communications, though this is beginning to change (see Appendix 2). If the

CEO's job is to establish a vision for everybody to follow, how can he or she know people have bought it and are following it, unless the process is measured?

Communications has been often held up as the glue of culture change, and yet very few big companies (GE, Xerox, British Air, among them) have really scored a major success in changing their cultures.[7] A few years ago, the author got an insight into the reason for the lack of success in changing, when reporting back to the CEO of a major Midwestern apparel manufacturer about how much communications effort and time would be necessary to bring real change. "I had no idea," was the CEO's reply. The change strategy turned into a video and disappeared, as did the CEO eventually.

3. Communications has long been perceived as a technical skill, not a strategic activity. Traditionally, public relations has been the profession that has staffed both internal and external corporate communications. Initially, this field was dominated by propagandists, publicists, and former newspaper reporters. Their jobs were very specialized—to get a name or product story in the press or keep a name or news story out of the press.

As time went on, the job of the corporate communicator began to expand to include producing newsletters, helping the advertising effort to sell a product, keeping track of public issues (such as environmental regulation, consumerism, and minority rights), selling the company on Wall Street, and managing crisis. When downsizing began in earnest in the United States in the early 1980s, the increasing strategic importance of these departments was often not recognized, as staffs were cut.

However, at the same time the world was becoming more interconnected via advanced communications technologies, and the potential for problems caused by communications flubs was increasing. The good news was that the CEO could, if he or she so wished, talk via videoconference to all employees in all locations at one time. The bad news was that the CEO could also be seen hesitating, fumbling, and making a back peddling statement on the 6 o'clock news. The stakes had been raised.

Into this communications void have marched all sorts of specialists— lawyers, human resource managers, and marketers—to manage communications in the place of the traditional technician or practitioner of public relations, which probably says more than anything else about the inability of communication practitioners to think strategically.

4. Senior managers have had a long-standing fear of a process they are afraid can't be totally controlled. Many senior managers have lived

happily under the illusion that they own the communications channels in their business—their newsletters, videos, and other missives to employees can always show the sun shining. This illusion helps keep alive the grapevine as a credible alternative to corporate manipulation of relevant information.

Some in senior management may find comfort in company newsletters that can talk about bowling scores and 20-year-service pins and not have to explain why the company is being sued by the EPA, why it has moved two plants to Juarez, or why the head of sales was fired. Also, the corporate newsletter may be irrelevant, but it's certainly a more attractive alternative to having to explain three straight down quarters to a 26-year-old general assignment reporter from the local newspaper. Even the annual report can be beautifully arranged to hide some ugly financial truths, such as top management compensation.[8]

## COMMUNICATIONS IS THE CEOs JOB

Times are changing, however. And there are a number of reasons why management has become willing to take some risks in communicating information. One reason is the necessity to respond to the challenges of the *public* marketplace. Public opinion today is driven by pictures on the television screen. News of insider trading, major plant closings, and failed products is no longer buried on the business pages; it is the stuff of daily television news shows. A world economy undergoing a sea change, such as is taking place at the close of the 20th century, is world class news, and the public is very concerned about the contributing events. CEOs and their financiers have exercised life and death powers over the economic vitality of many communities. At the same time, government continues to expand its regulatory impact on business through the Clean Air Act, trade and tariff provisions, securities and banking laws, and so on. New initiatives aimed at health care reform, and pension and benefit guarantees continue to work their way through public debate. Companies that ignore getting involved in public debate will be forced to live with the consequences.

Another reason why management is turning to communications is that U.S. business has restructured to an incredible degree. The consulting firm of Temple, Barker, and Sloan has predicted that through 1995, one out of five companies in the United States would restructure each year.

In the early 1990s, hundred of thousands of middle management jobs were eliminated.[9]

In earlier times, when management was more hierarchical, levels of middle management served primarily as information repackagers and gate-keepers to senior management. The move to drive responsibility down to line management, aided by the new technologies—especially personal computers, facsimile machines, and telecommunications—created a faster and more voluminous communications environment within the organization. As a result, information is potentially available to everyone inside— and often outside—the organization *on a real-time basis*. Because of this, decision making must be compressed to maintain competitive advantage.

Another result of restructuring is that the distance between top management and the lowest-level employee is narrowing. And employees, conditioned to getting information and explanations from world leaders in almost every field, including politics, sports, and entertainment, through television interviews, are making those expectations of their own management as well. Today's CEO, then, has a receptive audience to communicate a vision, and a new competitive environment that demands communication.

In addition, the new communications technologies are providing multiple channels for reaching internal and external audiences. But companies that have not encouraged a culture conducive to frequent and informal communication are not going to help foster it no matter how much technology they have.

## HOW CEOs CREATE VALUE WITH COMMUNICATION

A president's council, comprised of 15 plus Manville Corporation employees, representing the various business units and levels, meets regularly with the CEO to keep him from getting what he calls "CEO Disease," a disorder wherein the top executive has a warped view of what the troops are thinking because he talks only with top management.

"Our job is to make sure that no information gets filtered out, on the way up or on the way down," said one person on the council. The effort has proved so successful that members of Manville's board of directors have even taken to meeting with the council. One board member said he felt better about okaying a multimillion dollar expansion program at a Louisiana plant after talking to an hourly worker on the council. Noted the board member, "He (the employee) clearly understood that he had as much at stake in Manville's success as did shareholders." As a result, plant visits are now on the agenda of every board meeting.[10]

This unique communication process is helping create value for the organization. The process is providing management with an unfiltered read of the situation that reinforces the quantitative numbers. In addition, the emphasis on getting raw data from employees has also resulted in a new top-management policy of drop-ins at plants instead of the planned visits. Also, strategic goals are described in publications sent directly to employees' homes to avoid the filtering process of the office environment. A stamped, addressed envelope directly to the CEO provides a direct feedback loop. The council members are charged with reaching the wider group of employees to get a fix on issues that need to be brought up to the CEO. The only person quoted by name from these meetings is the CEO. As the business world moves to more highly integrated information technologies and organizations continue to flatten out, it will be more incumbent than ever to institute such reality checks. The more immediate value of the CEO and the board mixing with the troops is that it sets a strong example for other managers.

Some CEOs' approach to communication is interactive, as was that of Manville's. The approach used by others is more direct. "I'm not giving A's for effort. I'm giving A's for results," one exec was quoted as telling the troops. This straight-talk approach may better fit the times, though sometimes things might seem to get carried away. For example, Sears' CEO Edward A. Brennan was quoted at one meeting as saying the merchandise division could use a serious flushing out: "What we need right now is a can of Drano," he reportedly told the group. "We need to open the pipeline so we can have free conversations going both ways." The "Norman Schwarzkopf approach," as this directness was termed, was most exemplified in a famous meeting at IBM in 1991 when CEO John F. Akers reportedly complained angrily that too many people were standing around the office cooler and not out making sales calls. "Everyone is too comfortable at a time when the business is in crisis," he reportedly told the group.[11]

## VISION AND CULTURE

The CEO's responsibility is to state a clear and concise corporate vision and then aggressively communicate it to the constituencies that count—

shareholders, employees, and customers. The strong commitment made by many CEOs in recent years to link employees, quality, and customers is a story that has been told many times. In old-line industries under siege, such as manufacturing, retailing, banking, and even high technologies, such as electronics, CEOs have learned the value of *preaching*. In the 1980s, the message was "we have a good company, we are profitable, but the environment is changing and, therefore, we must change." Today the message is more pointed as competition becomes more global, fierce, and time-dependent. In some of the large *M* companies, such as IBM, GM, and 3M Company, senior management has realized that the only way to bring change to the culture is literally to reinvent the company. And so, new start-ups, like GM's Saturn, IBM's splintered business groups, and 3M's internal spinoffs have been instituted.

CEOs looking for a fast payoff on establishing and communicating vision are in for a surprise—*it takes a long time*. Then there are the problems of getting the message to employees through middle managers. It would probably not be an exaggeration to say that every internal corporate communication study ever done has concluded that employees want to get information directly from their managers. The problem is the same one a child has in playing post office: the message gets distorted as it is retold. It has been estimated that each time a message is communicated in an organization, 50 percent of its meaning is lost. Senior management has a powerful responsibility to get the company headed in the right direction. A vision developed with the involvement of employees and then aggressively and constantly communicated will win out. That was the inside story of saving Tylenol—the fact that managers were forced to continually analyze the company's hundred-year credo gave them a belief value that never hesitated when the chips were down. Contrast this with the culture of Salomon Brothers or Drexel Burnham, where original values and integrity were lost in the culture of individual greed [12] and resulting legal action for securities violations brought down Drexel and damaged the reputation of Salomon Brothers. The lack of strongly communicated and reinforced ethical values exacted costly tolls.

The approach of Manville in setting up direct dialogue with employees is one way in which top management can determine whether its message is getting through to employees. Walking the floors and buttonholing employees is one way. Another is to utilize publications that feature managers and employees involved in implementing the vision and telling their success story.

## THE VALUE OF VALUES

In the health care field, studies have shown that consumers prefer a religiously affiliated hospital because they feel that such a hospital will be more value-based. Likewise, the Mayo clinics are so well thought of, in part, because of a value system that posits patient concerns above all else.[13]

The beliefs or values of the organization support the CEO's vision. At Drexel, those values should have included integrity and honesty above all else. For government and the press, the overarching value is credibility. For a small start-up, the most important values might be faith and commitment. Visible symbols are also important in communicating values. The story is often told about how the Steuben Glass company breaks every imperfect piece of crystal that has even the smallest flaw. This delivers a clear message to customers and employees about the company's values.[14]

The purpose of many new value-driven kinds of internal communications is to show specifically by story and example the characteristics of this behavior and the outcome of its use. A story on workers visiting a customer's operation to better understand needs, a profile of a plant manager who lets workers vote on which colleagues should be on-the-job instructors, a story of how quality improved when union and management got together and set goals, how an employee's suggestion has resulted in greater output on a certain line are just a few of the kinds of stories that communicate the values associated with leadership, the quest for quality and greater profitability, and the empowerment of employees who want to improve the operation, and ultimately its profitability.

## GETTING THE WORDS OUT—TOOLS AND TECHNIQUES

The CEO communicates in everything he or she does—from the clothes worn, to the car driven, to the hours spent at the golf course. It is vital for a chief executive to be a walking billboard for the values of the organization. This also includes the CEO's role as a champion of communications. As the principal representative of the company, the chief executive represents the company before external as well as internal constituencies. This is a leadership role, not a management role. This role is very similar to that of the political leader—representing the organization to many constituencies: government, the community, top stockholders, regulators, major customers, and employees. If anything, this role will occupy more, not less, of the CEO's time in the future world of high-tech communications.

## Four Steps to Follow

Research from two national studies of CEOs concluded that there are four things a CEO should be doing to show leadership in communication:

1. *Developing a shared vision of the future*—knowing the needs and expectations of stakeholders, developing an  encompassing mission, and then communicating it.
2. *Establishing and maintaining trust in the organization's leader*—showing credibility and integrity.
3. *Initiating and managing change*—providing the monetary and human resources to get the job done.
4. *Empowering and motivating employees*—moving the organization away from authoritarian management to a culture of empowerment.[15]

## The CEO Creates Value

Open communication fostered by the CEO costs little, but it can create real value. Herman Miller, Inc., the Western Michigan-based maker of office furniture has an amazingly low absenteeism—between 1 percent and 2 percent—and realized $11.6 million in annual savings in five years with an employee suggestion program. Chairman Max DePree has fostered an open communications environment and a sense of equality in which employees feel empowered enough to go over the heads of managers to support the company's goals. Also, worker and senior management pay are more closely aligned.[16]

At the Toyota plant in Smyrna, Tennessee, empowerment has been redefined: any employee on the line can, at any time a problem arises, pull a cord that completely shuts down the line. A team quickly convenes to correct the problem and get the line up and running again.

If the CEO is the chief information officer of the organization, what ever happened to the head of corporate communications? That person is still there, but the job is now different; it is more directly linked to the mission of the organization. The corporate communications director helps senior management plan to communicate the vision. He or she also puts together the action plan that managers will use to communicate the message to all employees. For example, the manufacturing end of a large Midwestern food company wanted to do away with the traditional annual bonus and put its 8,000 hourly workers across the country on an incentive system to encourage productivity. Initially, the program had been poorly communicated and follow-up focus groups showed that in some plants the materials on the new program had never even been distributed. In order to remedy the situation, consultants recommended that a bare minimum of communications materials be developed, but greater effort be spent training plant managers and their personnel directors to understand the program and accept it so that they could enthusiastically sell it to workers. In this way, plant personnel were made a credible part of the communications process and were not just used as conduit.

### How to Do it

How should a leader communicate the corporate vision? Key factors in this effort include:

1. **Keep the message simple**. The length of the average soundbite on network television during the 1988 presidential election had dropped to 9.3 seconds from 42.3 seconds just 20 years earlier.[17]

In the media training that I have conducted for thousands of executives from around the country, I emphasize that the ability to deliver a simple, effective message in 20 to 30 seconds is paramount. It can be done with practice, and it is done best via simple pictures and stories. For example, George Bush's famous call to volunteerism asked for a "Thousand Points of Light." (It evolved into recognitions called "Point of Light" awards.)

2. **Use empathetic communications**. You must always put yourself in the listener's shoes. One of the major problems that the White House had in the minidepression of 1991–1992 was that it was out of touch with the plight of working people who were trying to make ends meet. Reportedly nobody on the White House staff had a real feeling for those who had been thrown out of work. For the CEO, it is incumbent to mix with employees to get good data on what they are thinking, what they are hearing from the grapevine, and how they really perceive you and what you're trying to do. No company would go into the marketplace without good consumer research. But how many launch an employee communications effort, even one as important as instituting a new vision, without the same kind of employee market data? Too many!

3. **Talk like you walk**. A CEO who takes home a giant salary when times are bad, who preaches holding down costs but lives like a king, who encourages innovation but never rewards it is not credible and will not be followed into battle.

4. **Paint the trucks**. One of the classic M.B.A. cases at Harvard for many years was the story of the utility that wanted to demonstrate and advertise that it had changed as a company. The symbol became painting the trucks, an act that has become a figure of speech for change agents. Visible symbols are crucial. Corporations spend millions of dollars annually on new corporate symbols because they want customers, the stock market, employees, and other constituencies to know that the status quo has been changed.

5. **Sell, sell, sell**. Implementing a corporate vision is difficult. It takes lots of time, and it involves persuasion skills. Sometimes you wonder how CEOs can so easily forget that many of them rose to the top because they were very good at selling themselves to others. If anything, that skill becomes more important in selling their idea of the future to internal constituencies. The process of communicating goals and visions throughout the organization requires the CEO's constant attention and involvement.

### System Changes

A CEO must visibly demonstrate that change is taking place. Beyond the obvious changing of symbols, the CEO must show that management supports changes in values. This will be visible in:

- A revised compensation and rewards system that links *everybody's* pay to performance.
- A recognition program that places a new emphasis on values such as innovation, quality, and customer service.
- An external communication program to customers, shareholders, and to the market in general that change is taking place.

### Suggestion Programs

One estimate has it that only one in 10 corporate CEOs can communicate effectively, talk candidly with employees, and encourage them to contribute new ideas.[18]

When Mattel CEO John Amerman asked employees to meet with him and give him suggestions to help turn around the company, the result was a series of work-team suggestions that helped the company rebound from a loss of $113 million in 1987 to an all-time earnings high of $91 million in 1990.[19] An employee suggestion program at Preston Trucking in Maryland resulted in 4,412 money-making ideas in one year. Average value to the company was $300 for each suggestion.[20]

## *Technologies For CEO Communications*

The variety of relatively new communications toys available to today's CEO is amazing:

- **Voice mail**—It's possible for the CEO to leave a voice mail message in every employee's mailbox. As this is being written, AT&T is introducing a low-cost picture phone capability that could allow the CEO to communicate one-on-one visually with an employee at his or her desk, or possibly one-way with all employees simultaneously.

- **E-mail**—Many companies where employees are constantly on the move set up an electronic mailbox (E-mail) that allows messages to be sent and retrieved via computer. CEOs can send messages to individuals or targeted groups anytime.

- **Video**—The 1980s saw an explosive growth in the use of video for communications. Video is far and away the most popular training medium. Video allows the CEO to deliver a clear and consistent message to all employees at any time. The video can also be packaged to deliver strategic corporate messages.

- **Tele/video conferencing**—Another popular communications tool for strategic messages has been large scale tele- or video-conferences, in which employees at diverse locations were brought together to simultaneously view a live corporate potlatch, or tribal reunion. The technology allows one-way, outbound video and two-way audio. It was very popular for annual state-of-the- company meetings, new product rollouts, and recognitions.

- **Brochures and newsletters**—The traditional communication medium for top management has been the monthly newsletter, quarterly magazine, or the annual report. Each serves a particular function and audience. There are a couple of downsides these days to using this kind of medium—people today view more than they read, *and* corporate management continues to be paranoid about what it puts in print. When a company tells only good, positive news, it loses credibility and the grapevine grows.

* **Comfortable shoes**—There are many kinds of very comfortable shoe styles available today to help the CEO get through a day of walking around talking to employees.

### Measuring Impact

"How do you know that what you do works?" is an often-asked question of communicators. Why this question should be so mysterious seems odd in this day of sophisticated marketing research.

When the CEO communicates a vision, that CEO has a right—and an obligation—to see if the vision is having the desired impact.

Communications for Management, Inc. International has developed a communications evaluation model containing three major components:

1. Flow—how easily the message gets where it's going.
2. Content—what the message is saying.
3. Impact—what the outcome of the message is.

Measuring the impact of the CEO's communications efforts can be formal and informal. An informal measure might simply consist of walking around at various locations to discover, by random conversation with employees, the extent to which they understand a program.

More formal evaluation techniques are necessary to discover specifically whether people are actually accepting the process. Using standard survey research, we can develop an evaluation instrument that can pinpoint at just what level of acceptance employees are with regards to the CEO's message.

Sound evaluation techniques can measure whether employees are only *aware* of the corporate message or whether they are actually committed to it and show this commitment through behaviors that contribute to the bottom line—like the productivity increases. This makes a big difference.

As U.S. management streamlines and downsizes its operations, it has broken a long-standing contract that rewarded loyalty with longevity. Companies with a strong culture of avoiding layoffs, like Digital Equipment, IBM, and Kraft, have done just the opposite. Researchers maintain that the long-term outcome will be evolution of a new type of employee who is no longer loyal to the company, but only to his or her own career. Getting to that employee with a new corporate vision will not be easy.

## SUMMARY

This is not an easy time to be a CEO. Corporate boards and major shareholder groups are becoming more assertive. The media is criticizing executive compensation plans: vis-a-vis, performance and senior management are constantly being compared to the Japanese model. The public is watching for missteps, and employees are more cynical than ever.

Continuous, credible communication of a strategic message to the corporation's stakeholders is the way out of the bag. The way you move the organization forward today is not the way you did it before. Those who see this and adapt will be successful; the others are in harm's way.

## ENDNOTES

1. John P. Kotter, "What Leaders Really Do," *Harvard Business Review*, May/June 1990, p. 103.
2. Alan Farnham, "The Trust Gap," *Fortune*, December 4, 1989, pp. 56–78.
3. *Ibid*.
4. Steve Lohr, "Pulling Down the Corporate Clubhouse," *New York Times*, April 12, 1991, p. 3–1.
5. J. David Pincus, Robert E. Bayfield, and J. Nicholas DeBonis, "Transforming CEOs into Chief Communications Officers," *Public Relations Journal*, November 1991, p. 26.
6. Quoted in James W. Singer, "Behind the New Aggressiveness," *National Journal*, August 16, 1980, p. 1367.
7. Keith H. Hammonds, "Why Big Companies Are So Tough to Change," *Business Week*, June 17, 1991, p. 28.
8. Amanda Bennett, "Top Officer's Pay Can Be Hard to Figure Out without a Calculator and Lots of Sifting," *The Wall Street Journal*, June 21, 1991, p. B1.
9. K. Lochridge and M. Bickerstaff, "The Restructuring Puzzle: Ways to Make the Pieces Fit," Presentation at the 1991 American Society for Training and Development National Conference in San Francisco.

10. Claudia H. Deutsch, "Call It 'CEO Disease,' Then Listen," *New York Times*, December 15, 1991, p. 23.

11. Gabriella Stern, "As the Going Gets Tougher, More Bosses Are Getting Tough with Their Workers," *The Wall Street Journal*, June 18, 1991, p. B1.

12. For a more extended treatment of the fall of Drexel Burnham, see James B. Stewart, *Den of Thieves* (New York: Simon & Schuster, 1991) and Richard D. Hylton, "Salomon's Remaining Challenges," *New York Times*, August 19, 1991, p. C1.

13. Daniel J. Beckham, "Everyday Values," *Healthcare Forum*, March/April 1991, pp. 34-38.

14. Robert L. Dilenschneider, "A Briefing for Leaders, Communications as the Ultimate Exercise of Power," Bristol, Vt.: Soundview Executive Book Summaries, October 1991.

15. Pincus, Bayfield, and DeBonis, "Transforming CEOs into Chief Communications Officers," p. 23.

16. Joani Nelson-Horchler, "The Magic of Herman Miller," *Industry Week*, February 18, 1991, pp. 11-17.

17. K. Adatto, "TV Tidbits Starve Democracy," *New York Times*, December 10, 1989, p. 23.

18. Faye Rice, "Champions of Communications," *Fortune*, June 3, 1991, pp. 111-120.

19. *Ibid*.

20. Farnham, "The Trust Gap," p. 70.

## Chapter Three

# Managing Communications

Telecommunications and information technology, population growth, and new ideas about managing have all impacted how companies communicate. Traditionally, communication management has spoked out from a small corporate staff office. Corporate communication today encompasses activities at many levels of the organization, and all the indicators point to increased decentralization in the near future.

The history of corporate communications activities has been erratic—some companies have done an excellent job over the years in communicating to internal and external audiences: employees, customers, shareholders, the community, government agencies, and the public. But, communications was often seen as a narrow staff function involved with employee relations. Public relations people handled publicity or damage control with the press. The jobs were always fairly small and the focus was on the tactical (doing newsletters, answering press calls, making films, writing speeches, planting stories) rather than on strategic issues.

Beginning in the 1960s, business, like society's other institutions, began to lose credibility and came under closer public scrutiny. A skeptical public became active in calling for more government regulation of pollution, civil rights, products, safety, and the like. During this period the importance of dealing with external audiences began to grow. But with big problems and small nonstrategic staffs outside public relations firms began assuming a greater role in providing strategy and reach for the communications function. Today, as companies downsize and flatten out their organizational charts, corporate communication is focusing more on employees, and corporate public relations is involved more in marketing.

Because of the increasing importance of communications, specialists from other fields, such as attorneys and marketers, are filling top public relations slots in many companies. Part of the reason is that corporate communicators are still not perceived as having strategic skills.

Whether the corporate communications function remains large or small, in-house or with agencies, centralized or pushed out into the field, properly staffed or not, a large number of communications responsibilities for the organization still remain to be accomplished.

Those responsibilities include:

1. Communications strategy—Providing senior management with the internal and external communications perspective on how communication can be used to create value.

2. Issues management—Tracking and providing strategy for influencing the outcome of potential external actions that may impact the organization.

3. Strategic support—Back-up services such as speechwriting, video production, corporate advocacy, takeover defense, and other materials directly in support of top-management actions.

4. Government relations—Representing the organization before state, federal, legislative, and regulatory bodies.

5. Media relations—Managing the organization's relations with local, state, regional, national, and international media.

6. Marketing public relations—Direct support of the marketing effort with strategy, public relations, product publicity, and collateral materials.

7. Consumer relations—Managing the organization's direct contact program with customers to provide information, to answer questions, and to assist with media aspects of recall efforts.

8. Crisis communications—Strategic and tactical management of the communications tied directly to activation of a corporate crisis plan.

9. Financial investor relations—Activities designed to meet legal requirements to inform shareholders and the market of "material" information impacting the organization. Also includes setting up analyst briefings, producing quarterly and annual reports, and handling media calls.

10. Interest group liaison—Management of the organization's contacts with public interest groups that regularly monitor and comment on the organization's activities.

11. Community relations—Activities designed to build goodwill and support among residents living in proximity of corporate operations.

12. Employee communications—Supporting senior management and human resources responsibilities for communicating with employees.

## PROFESSIONAL QUALIFICATIONS

*"Any dumbbell, nitwit or crook can call himself a*
*public relations practitioner."*
-Edward L. Bernays, the
father of public relations[1]

Unlike more policed and regulated professions, such as law, medicine, engineering, and even management, the field of communications—public relations, journalism (including "TV-anchordom"), and so on—does not have widely recognized professional criteria.

The two major professional communicators associations, the Public Relations Society of America (PRSA) and International Association of Business Communicators (IABC), do have certifications: Accredited in Business Communications (*ABC* for IABC members) and Accredited in Public Relations (*APR* for PRSA members), but not many outside the field know about it. And rarely, unless there is an active society member doing the hiring, will it ever come up as a criterion for recruiting or in a job interview.

Formerly, communications jobs went to journalists who wanted to escape poor pay, long hours, and the pressures of newspapering. But as communication and information have become bigger issues in U.S. society and the stakes have raised, top management in many firms has decided the job is too important to be left to journalists and, in many instances, top positions have gone to specialists in law, finance, marketing, and administration.

The general background for a person going into communications is a basic ability to write clearly on a number of subjects. Another skill high on the list, traditionally, has been a background as a reporter. Certainly, the person who handles external communications benefits from that background. Dealing with the media is not for amateurs. Since even the highest-paid, sharpest communicators can stumble, it is important to have someone who can interact with both senior management and the media. Lawyers and M.B.A.s normally aren't qualified for this kind of work, unless they have a journalism background. An ex-reporter has the instincts to know where the media is "coming from"—what they want, how fast they need it, and even how the company is likely to fare in the story.

## EVOLVING RESPONSIBILITIES

In the past, the communications program was more tactical than strategic. The job had certain functions: support human relations activities such as blood drives and United Way, and build a sense of goodwill by doting on the personal accomplishments of employees. The job of the public relations department was reactive—shielding executives from the press, producing the annual report, writing an occasional speech, and publishing the monthly newsletter.

Few, if any, of the communications department's responsibilities were directed towards helping accomplish the corporate mission. Also, public relations people suffered from the centuries old prejudice against the messenger of bad tidings. The public relations department was the link to the outside world. If something bad got reported in the press, it was their fault. On the flip side, the public relations director was also perceived as a fixer who could perform magic with the press, turning a sow's ear into a silk purse, or at least making a mediocre CEO into a *wunderkind*.

When the public-interest groups started going after companies 20 years ago for issues relating to civil rights, the environment, consumers, and other problems, companies realized they were in a new ball game and they began to become more aggressive in their communication. This coincided with the growth of the mass media and higher visibility that came with these public issues. At the same time, the cost for not recognizing these changes went up as well. For example, missteps on consumer issues by Ford and Firestone helped doom products like the Pinto and the 500 radial tire. Management took steps to deal with this new environment: training managers to handle media interviews, strengthening government relations activities, becoming more involved in the local community and with organizations impacted by the company, and keeping better track of upcoming issues.[2]

In an earlier time, it might have been said that financial communications, product publicity, and customer relations were all tied to the economic mission of the firm, while press relations, employee communications, and community relations were not directly tied to the economic mission. (See

**FIGURE 3-1**
*Traditional Communications Staffing Structure*

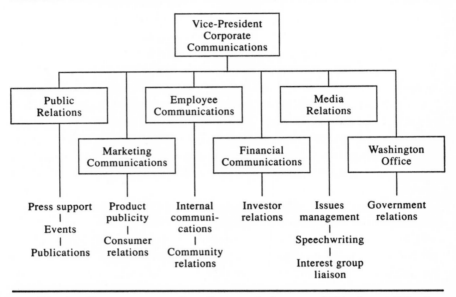

A traditional staffing structure centralizes all communication responsibilities in a staff function. Today, the new approach is to spread these functions out among staff offices, as in the case of public relations (marketing) or internal communications (human resources) or send responsibility to a lower level (division, Plant Manager).

Figure 3–1.) As the business environment changed in the last decade, this is no longer the case.

The issue today is perception—how the company is perceived by the publics it must deal with. Today, such people as *environmental consumers* and *concerned investors* hold the company to various health and quality and moral standards.

## COMMUNICATION STRATEGY

A corporation has few legal mandates to communicate other than some basic government rules to protect shareholders. How, why, when, and to whom an organization communicates must come from a management realization that communication contributes to the mission of that organization. In today's environment, a company that does not communicate to a wide number of constituencies will end up hurting its financial prospects. Companies like Coca-Cola and IBM, with long established policies of avoiding the media, learned that such policies can impact sales negatively in the information-driven business environment and made adjustments. Holdouts like Proctor and Gamble have paid the price (see Chapter 9).

Communication strategy is the game plan of a company for getting the word out to its audiences. The strategy spells out *who* those audiences are, *why* communicating with them is important, *when* and *where* communication should take place, *who* is responsible for communications, *what* should be said, and *what* the linkage is to business goals. But the most important part of communications strategy is the communications *environment* that top management creates. To be effective, top management must take the lead in communication planning.

Organizations concerned about mission, vision, and values need to develop their strategy based on specific message platforms derived from those missions, visions, and the values. Those messages must be specified for each targeted audience and delivered continuously. The CEO is no longer just a manager; he or she is a *visionary*.

As Figure 3-2 indicates, the classic communication strategy model is a closed loop so that constant improvements can be made.

The communications model does not operate in a vacuum. It starts with the strategic goals of the organization. The business strategy, based on the mission statement, explains how the company will define its success. The strategic role of communication will be to assist internally, by motivating employees to productive action, and externally, by helping position the company with external audiences. (See Figure 3-3.)

## ORGANIZING AND STAFF

The communications executive has three major responsibilities: (1) consultation, (2) assistance, and (3) management. Above all else, he or she is a *consultant* to top management. Questions like, How are we going to handle this takeover attempt? or How do we break this news to the employees? or How can we turn this story around? are presented to the communications executive for ideas.

The same manager provides assistance using internal and external resources to put together the pieces that will form a strategy—from speeches

**FIGURE 3–2**
*Strategic Communications Model*

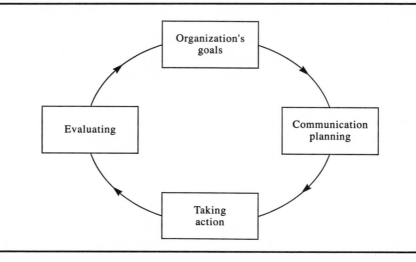

to annual reports, to product publicity campaigns, to community relations programs.

The *management* responsibility of the communications executive is to staff and execute a plan, evaluate its effectiveness, and develop improvements. The size of the communications department is determined by its mission. In some of today's Fortune 500 companies (like GE), where responsibility has been totally pushed down into the organization, corporate communications is minimal in size. At other more traditionally organized companies like Westinghouse, the number can run to 50 or more.

In most companies, the communications program is centralized at the vice-presidential level, and overall policy direction is usually at corporate headquarters. Communications personnel are often stationed close to marketing operations, near the New York financial markets or in Washington for governmental work.

Communications programs have no hard and fast rules pertaining to either size or location. Some industries, like insurance, because of the nature of their business, need large centralized communication staffs, with large budgets. New technologies and decentralized organizational structures point to little or no growth in the future, but more effective use of communications technologies.

**FIGURE 3–3**
*Organizational Strategy*

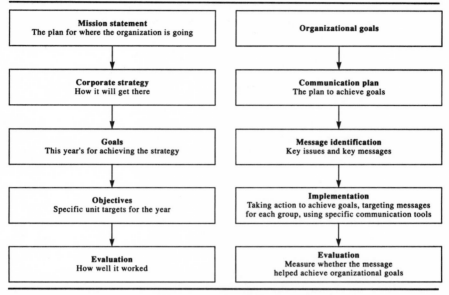

A comparison of organizational strategy and corporate communications strategy.

## REORGANIZING THE COMMUNICATIONS FUNCTION

Corporate communicators are looking for new ways to serve the new flattened U.S. organization. Southern California Edison and Ontario Hydro have reorganized their communications departments so that internal corporate clients are assigned a single account executive, much like is done in an ad agency. That executive is responsible for dealing with all the technical specialists on staff and with vendors to accomplish the project. The most important aspect of this new approach is that it positions the communications person to be involved in a project from the beginning. "To be successful communicators," said Lew Phelps, Edison's vice president of corporate communications, "we must position ourselves ahead of the curve."[3] And to get ahead of the curve requires account executive communicators with a sense of where the business is going. (See Figure 3–4.)

Ontario Hydro went to the new structure after executives expressed frustration at having to deal with numerous contacts in the corporate relations branch. They wanted a high-level communication strategist to help give them advice, and to plan and manage project services. Both companies use contracts to spell out how communications will be used to achieve business objectives. Other issues they consider are budgets, evaluation, key messages, and tracking.

## FINANCING CORPORATE COMMUNICATIONS

Because costs of public relations activities vary greatly, financing of the function varies as well. In some situations, services are provided to all units and charged to corporate overhead. In others, each profit center receives a charge-back, sometimes based on a percentage of sales produced by the unit. In a third situation, each profit center assumes charge of its own communications activities. And finally, there are situations in which each profit center is charged back either the out-of-pocket costs for each project or the actual cost, which includes salaries and overhead. This arrangement creates a situation in which the profit center might argue successfully that it should be able to use an outside firm. Depending on what kind of product and consumer public relations are involved, the financing becomes a debatable point. For the bulk of *corporate* assignments involving overall corporate image, however, location and control remain centralized at headquarters.

Costs associated with running an in-house communications program are normally limited to salaries, overhead, and direct costs for outside services. Capital expenses are minimal. One of the major distinctions between advertising/marketing and communications is costs. Most communication activities use "free" channels of dissemination—magazine stories, newspapers, radio, TV—as opposed to bought space. The biggest problem here is that not enough is spent evaluating the results of the program. The consensus of researchers is that about 10 percent of any communications program cost should be spent on evaluation.

Today, one of the more common systems is to determine what the hourly cost of operation is and bill out services to the division. Overhead is usually figured at twice the total cost of salaries and is normally determined by adding the costs of the people involved. For comparison purposes, it might be noted that most outside public relations counsel bill at three times the hourly rate they pay their employees, plus expenses. Competent in-house public relations professionals will be able to estimate billable hours and

**FIGURE 3–4**
*Client-Specific Communication Department*

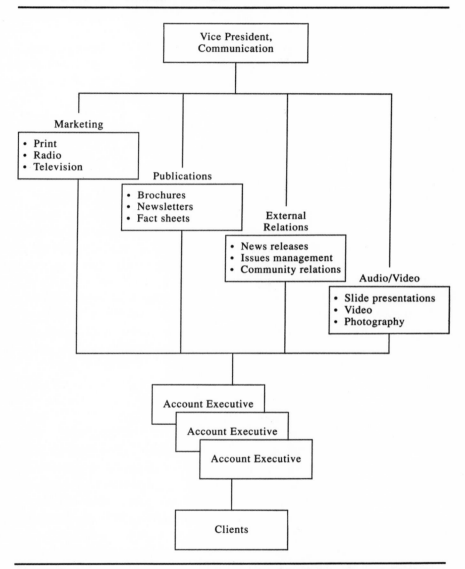

The account executive communications support model is designed to support a more decentralized organization.

expenses in advance of a project with a reasonable amount of accuracy. Submission of daily time sheets, which log fractions of an hour worked on specific activities, will help track costs. This method further serves in employee evaluation.

A good plan, especially for a large project, will also be organized on a time-line chart. It should be remembered that there are certain communications functions that are difficult to track, especially the fire-fighting kinds of public relations often demanded in a crisis situation.

## SPEECHWRITING

Many large corporations employ full-time speechwriters. Executive speeches range from significant, thought-provoking, policy-setting, and newsworthy, all the way to hackneyed, cliche-filled Babbitry. Speeches should play to the audience at hand and to the interests of the public. A good speech writer makes suggestions based on current ideas and trends. One approach for attracting attention is to do a speech that runs against the tide of what others are saying.

An effective approach is for the executive and the speechwriter to sit down together and prepare a press release first, rather than an outline of the talk, to force themselves to concentrate on content and impact. Such a technique also gives the executive a chance to see in what direction the speech is going.

## TACTICAL SUPPORT

One of the great concerns in communications today is that communicators are too often perceived as tactical—makers of things—and not strategic. The perception is often accurate. Many communicators have strategic portfolios but prefer to work on newsletters. We do not intend to denigrate the tactical aspects of the business, but the movement in recent years is to farm this work out to vendors, and reposition corporate communicators for strategic work. This will be a painful process because so many communicators lack the necessary perspective.

Change in audio-visual technology to support communication has been impressive. Desktop computers that can produce anything from a typeset daily news summary to four-color brochures ready for printing are becoming common. Video technology that can give any employee the ability to document training and edit a video program on a disk is also now available in high-quality formats. New multimedia technology will soon integrate video and computer software at the employee's desk. At the same time, companies are farming out more of this effort while looking to their communications staffs for strategic planning and management help.

## COMMUNITY RELATIONS

In some industries, community issues are very important. Examples include areas where the organization is a dominant employer or where the organization's operations pose potential safety and environmental concerns, such as with a waste incinerator.

Part of a communication manager's function is to help identify new bumps in the community's economic and social fabric, and to bring them to management's attention. Important strategies include making the community comfortable with the facility through tours, open houses, participation by managers in community activities, and developing relationships with local influentials.

The important thing is that there is one-on-one interaction between company officials and the people in the community. (Chapter 7 provides additional information on dealing with community groups.)

## OUTSIDE HELP

More than ever before, organizations are using outside services to bolster the communication function. A number of vertically integrated communication firms provide almost every imaginable service from writing simple news releases, to launching a new product, to measuring employee attitudes, to helping get a bill through Congress.

Smart companies today break up projects to get the most cost-effective services possible. Usually, the outside firm that handles a national product rollout is not going to be competitive on managing an open house. Also, public relations firms have reputations for certain kinds of specialty work—Hill & Knowlton for governmental work, Burson-Marsteller for marketing communications, and so on. Many smaller, local firms can help with activities like training, auditing, doing publications, making videos, and the like.

In the next chapter, we will look at employee communications, possibly the most important company communication responsibility of the 1990s.

## SUMMARY

Managing an organization's communications activities is not easy. There are many audiences and much work to do. Couple this with the multiplication of communication technologies and channels, and the job is formidable. Few organizations today have all the communication activities centralized in one umbrella department. We sometimes see internal communication in human resources, external communication in the legal department, and public relations in marketing. Though decried by leaders in the public relations field, this situation attests to the growing importance of the profession and the slowness of professionals in catching up to the new realities.

## ENDNOTES

1. Alvin M. Hattal, "The Father of Public Relations: Edward L. Bernays," *IABC Communication World*, January 1992, p. 14.
2. H.W. Close, "Public Relations as a Management Function," *Public Relations Journal*, March 1980, pp. 19–20.
3. Kevin Lennon and Keith A. Sheldon, "From Canada to California: New Directions in Corporate Communication," *IABC Communication World*, January 1992, pp. 42–45.

## Chapter Four

# Communicating with Employees

The economists can easily describe the problem. To create value, they say, you must effectively allocate resources—money, time, materials, methods, and people. The knowledge to marshall, move, and deploy money, time, materials, and methods is available everywhere around the globe. The abilities of its *people* are the only unique resource that a U.S. company or any company anywhere brings to the world market today. It is the allocating of these human resources wherein the great business opportunities and challenges exist for the future.

It has been estimated by Peter Drucker[1], among others, that 10 percent to 20 percent of an organization's actions produce 80 percent to 90 percent of the results. We might conclude, then, that management has learned to effectively manage all the resources except the human one.

This realization that people are the least effectively allocated resource, shown by the successful Japanese example, is changing how companies are organizing and managing themselves in the 1990s. Quality circles, self-directed work groups, emphasis on mission/vision/values, customer-driven initiatives are all manifestations of this drive to make the actions of an organization's human resources count for more.

In organizations where management has continued to view people only as a *cost*, the process of improving their contribution to value is not moving forward. But in other organizations, systems that impact the performance of people—compensation, recognition, motivation, development, and communication, among others—are being looked at more closely today in an effort to create additional value for the organization.

In today's organization, the CEO spends about 20 percent of his or her time on human resources issues. Current human resources issues of major CEO concern are productivity improvement and employee communications. More effective employee communication is seen as a means to enhance productivity and impart an understanding of organizational goals. In addition, top priorities such as cost reduction, product quality, and customer service have important communication components.[2]

This chapter looks at what changes can be introduced to help contribute to the more effective deployment of human resources through better management communication.

Our thesis is that when employee communication is focused on achieving corporate mission, this creates value. Further, we believe this linkage between behavior and value creation is often missed by management. We are going to focus on the proposition that good communication is not a nice-to-do, but a got-to-do.[3]

## THAT OLD-TIME RELIGION

*"Every time I pass through these gates, I leave my rights as a free man. I spend nine hours in there, in prison, and then come out into my country again."*

The words of Bob Cratchet to his Uncle Ebeneezer in the 19th century? The quote of a prisoner on work release? A soldier at a bar off base? Not at all. These are the remarks of an employee at the General Motors plant in Lordstown, Ohio.[4]

These are the words of someone who's part of the classic model of authoritarian corporate organization. And certainly, when the ranks of U.S. business were filled by returning soldiers after World War II, this management style meshed neatly with military traditions.

The climate of the authoritarian organization is an arbitrary and inflexible hierarchical structure, consisting of the withholding of information from subordinates and a closed door to upward communications. Withholding information is a classic way to maintain power. Because information is hoarded and not shared with the worker, the grapevine takes over as the primary source of information.

The authoritarian model is characteristic of slower-growth companies. Slipping credibility, poor linkage between pay and performance, and little emphasis on quality of work are also characteristics of these companies. In faster-growth companies, the opposites can be seen, including greater respect for employees and value from their involvement, linkage between pay and performance, with higher rewards for better performers, and an emphasis on quality and a more participative management style. Each of these cultures supports different levels of productivity and profitability.[5]

Recognition that the old-time religion doesn't work began 20 years ago when the United States started losing its footing in manufacturing, and proprietary technology jobs began to move off-shore. Productivity started to slide and customer loyalty turned to imports. The writings of management gurus like Deming, Crosby, Juran, and others started taking hold as managers began to see the benefits of a new work model that was the hallmark of the Japanese miracle.

A major aspect of the Japanese model was that it was *participatory*: employee circles were organized to solve problems on the shop floor. Responsibility for decision making was shared by employee and supervisor. Manufacturing companies in the United States began to copy this model. The organization was flattened—layers of middle management were thrown out, and the words *quality* and *customer focus* became part of the business vocabulary. Organizations had to have a strategic plan supported by a vision, a mission, and values in order to succeed. As these new business ideas began to take hold in organizations in the United States, old-time managers began bumping into some walls. First of all, the old authoritarian type of management didn't work in an environment of shared decision making.

At the same time, the work force was changing. The stable work force of the postwar era disappeared. Today's employee population includes soon-to-be retirees from that era, aging boomers, mid-career people, Hispanics, highly educated women, high-tech specialists, and entrepreneurs.[6]

The challenge is now to prepare these employees for a less stable work environment, motivate them to find job satisfaction as well as real pay, and do more face-to-face communicating.

Also, there were changes in society. U.S. institutions, including business, were under attack by a new generation bent on change. In addition, in the early 1990s, massive cutbacks and restructurings occurred in the wake of the gilded '80s, when the bill came due for companies that had taken on excessive debt and were now being forced to become more efficient. Coupled with massive changes in communications technologies, the inexorable move towards a new management model was inevitable.

With new information technologies such as television, computers, satellites, and telecommunications, employees were receiving information in real time, and the edge that management enjoyed in hoarding information no longer existed. As senior management began advocating worker participation, the hierarchy began to crumble like an Eastern European duchy, and empowered workers began demanding more equity.

The new model was now *leadership*, not *management*. Management was impersonal, but leadership was personal. Employees yearned to know that management loved them as much as it loved profits. Employee views of top management were found to impact performance more strongly than almost anything else including salary, supervisor, policies, and even co-workers.[7] The medium of this personal style is and always has been communication.

But well-managed organizations had always had good employee communications. Nearly a half century ago, GE put together a mission for employee relations.[8] Even further back, when Arthur Page joined AT&T in 1927 to become public relations vice president, he pushed for a communications system that would emphasize upward and downward communications.[9] Studies by all the major human resource consulting firms have shown time and again that employees prefer to find out about their organization from their own supervisors, not from the grapevine.

Research has continued to show that employees in the United States are better informed these days, and communication is more direct, honest, and relevant to their work; yet there has been no directed effort on the part of management to identify the linkage between behavior and the strategic plan.[10]

A national study of workers' attitudes by the Wyatt Co. showed most firms are good *at* talking at their workers. About 80 percent of the 5,836 full-time and 798 part-time workers who took part in the study said they understood their company's goals. But just 38 percent said employers seek out their views and suggestions. That number is down from 42 percent in 1989. And less than one third said their employers do a good job of involving workers in decisions that affect them. Only one out of four workers said their company did a good job of explaining the reasons behind their decisions, and only one third of the managers agreed they did a good job of explaining decisions.[11]

Some companies have responded well to the new reality, accepting change and retraining managers for the new work environment. Others have used the right words—mission, vision, values, change, performance—but, in fact have not shown it in their actions. Communication without credibility doesn't work. In the wake of massive cutbacks announced by GM, employees began to realize that despite good intentions and good communication and willingness to change, bad management decisions count for more than all the communication in the world.

## COMMUNICATION AND THE NEW CLIMATE

Leaders today have been forced to look at some tough questions about communication:

1. Can we have a good corporate image if we don't have a good internal image among our own people?
2. If an employee is not informed and loyal, and as a result, does not exercise good judgment, how much impact could this have on the economic mission?
3. Will we have the capability to give employees the wide range of information they need—all the way from safety to equal employment?
4. Can we have a quality program without better communication?

Part of the new interest in communications is attributable to expanded employee participation in decision making. Employees, who now often define their lives in terms of their work, have higher expectations for participation.

Studies over the past 20 years have shown that employees have very simple communications wants. They want to know what the problems are, how the company is going to deal with them, and what their employee roles are. And they want to hear about this from somebody who knows what's going on—preferably their immediate supervisor.[12] In the absence of credible communication, the grapevine will fill the gap. The grapevine gives them a real, live person who seems to know what's going on.[13] Educated employees want even more information. They not only want to know *what*; they want to know *why*.

The questions arise: Why isn't there trust between management and employees? Why does management withhold information? Several reasons have been put forward:

- Giving away information means giving away power.
- Somehow the competition will get hold of the information.
- Giving out information takes time.

Factors that build trust include openness, feedback, congruity, autonomy, and shared values.[14]

Line managers, more than anybody else, need to break through the authoritarian model. All the excellence models talk about getting rid of the visible management perks like the parking space. They talk about

---

**Box 4–1**

In the new work environment, key mesages must be communicated:

1. "This is our mission . . . and here's how you fit in."
2. "What you do here is important."
3. "Let me tell you how you're doing."
4. "Let me help you do your job better."
5. "We'll help you with your personal problems."
6. "Here's how our unit did this quarter."
7. "We made a mistake, but here's how we're going to fix it."
8. "What are your ideas?"

---

management by walking around, about communication with employees on neutral ground—on the shop floor, in the hallway, and even in the restrooms. Studies show most managers are poor listeners. According to Russ Miller of TPF&C, the biggest problem is ongoing maintenance and continuation of managerial communication. When managers only talk with workers during crises, workers begin to doubt the sincerity of vows of concern.[15]

## COMMUNICATIONS AND PROFITS

It's an old question: Can you link communication with profitability? This is a question that many skeptical managers continue to ask. The Weyerhauser Company did a study of its plants and found that its most profitable operations had the most open and effective communications channels.

The internal study concluded this:

Research and experience show that employees are most highly motivated and make their greatest contribution to the business when there is full and open communication at work. The evidence also shows that where there is an adequate flow of information and ideas among employees, productivity is enhanced and confusion, duplication, and unproductive conflict are minimized. Further, because improving communication requires no capital, the productivity gains that result become total profit.

Weyerhauser's study revealed a number of substantive findings that can be applied in any organization:

1. Build a positive communications climate. Doing this involves several assumptions:
   a. Each employee in the unit is a member of the same team, with the right to hear and be heard on things that affect the group.
   b. Talking about issues and problems is more helpful than not talking about them.
   c. An information void in areas of employee interest will be quickly filled with misinformation through the grapevine.

One plant manager noted:

We have found employees are very interested in plant detail, not only how it works, but how it's doing. They want to see comparative information on a day-to-day basis. . . . This kind of detail . . . makes people interested in their jobs rather than just putting in time.

Weyerhauser's study concluded that another key was upward communications—hotlines, crew meetings, suggestion systems, attitude surveys, and so on. This was consistent with the company's feelings that workers wanted more control over their jobs.

Supervisors at some mills got rid of their perks—white hats, reserved parking, separate offices, and so on. They wanted to be accessible. One plant conducted regular communication meetings where rotating representatives from each group sat down with the assistant mill manager and other management representatives on a weekly basis for an exchange of information, ideas, and feelings about the operation. With certain exceptions, such as personnel matters, anything could be discussed: profit and loss statements, sales statistics, production plans, cost items, feedback, supervisory practices, and so on. Minutes from each meeting, along with management responses, were circulated throughout the mill.

2. Define management responsibilities. The report laid out three areas that managers must be responsible for:
   a. Provide clear communication of what must be accomplished and what is expected of employees. For example, if a customer is having a problem with a product, everyone who can impact improvement is involved in solving the problem.
   b. Provide feedback on how employees meet management's expectations, and give a timely, candid response to employee questions and concerns. (Some experts suggest that feedback must be specific, given as soon as possible, saved for key payoff areas, and provide employees with key information they can use to improve performance.)

    *c.* Provide information to do the job. As the company moves decision making to lower levels and attempts to expand the scope of supervisory responsibilities, Weyerhauser discovered information needs of everyone increase at all levels. The rule of thumb, then, the company concluded, was to ask Who else needs to know about this?

3. Support supervisors. Supervisors at Weyerhauser told management they were very interested in being informed about:

    *a.* Short-term operating objectives and production plans.

    *b.* Actual or anticipated changes in plant policies, procedures, or products.

    *c.* Long-term plans for the operation.

    *d.* How business is doing.

    *e.* How other shifts are doing.

    *f.* Success of the product at end sale.

One manager in the study discovered that because his supervisors had never had a clear explanation of the work agreement, all answers to employee questions about the union contract had to come from the shop steward. He remedied this by bringing in labor attorneys for both union and management so that everyone would have a clear understanding of the situation.

4. Communicate with work groups. After studying communications at both profitable and unprofitable plants, the report concluded that "one trademark of the leading units visited . . . was frequent and regular opportunities for face-to-face communications between people in work groups whose functions are related . . . often these meetings require as little as fifteen to twenty minutes." One plant reportedly reduced its costs by more than a million dollars annually through better communications between two departments. If a meeting is clearly focused, the report concluded, it can be a money and time saver, not a waster.

Each of the profitable plants had, at minimum, a low-budget newsletter photocopied on 8.5 x 11-inch paper. An employee communications committee with representatives from each department helped the part-time editor distribute it. Members of the communications committee wore press stickers on their hard hats, and other employees fed them information. Typical stories they wrote about included:

- Changes in plant procedures.
- New hires.
- Safety reports.
- Production figures.

- "Well dones."
- Capital project progress.
- Business outlook.
- Employee questions/management answers.

New employee orientation was both general and specific. "It's the best time to communicate," said one official. "It's the only time when we have his undivided attention." The general orientation includes an audio-visual presentation about the company and its mission, a presentation on company-employee relationships (pay practices, benefits, expectations), the relationship of the company to the community, and an overview of the region the employee is working in.

The specific orientation covered plant management, organization and philosophy, unit processes and procedures, introduction to supervisors and co-workers, explanation of the union contract, communications channels, and specifics of the job, and why it exists. The whole thrust of the presentation is from the employee's perspective.[16]

## SCRIPT FOR A DIALOGUE

What should managers discuss with employees? If you look at some corporate publications, you might think the topics are birthdays and bowling scores. But actually, there are at least a half-dozen crucial topics that must be discussed regularly:

1. *The mission of the unit*—Employees are more concerned with their own division than with the company in general.[17]

2. *What the employee's responsibilities are*—Employees want to know the criteria by which they will be judged, and what they are expected to do. Much of this can be accomplished during orientation on the first day of work, a time when the employee is most impressionable. Orientation should be better utilized than it currently is in many companies.

3. *Feedback on performance*—In more and more companies, compensation is being linked more frequently to performance and less to seniority. Employees need feedback on a frequent basis. The *annual* performance review is not enough to maintain an employee's motivation. Performance feedback should be continuous, even weekly, so that when the annual evaluation is made, there are no surprises. Continuous dialogue on perfor-

mance can also lead to short- and long-term strategies for employee development.

4. *Individual needs and concerns*—Smart companies understand today that personal problems can impact job performance. Consequently, they have developed employee-assistance programs to help with problems such as substance abuse, economic problems, and family difficulties. Supervisors must be trained to identify these problems and get help for the employee when necessary

5. *Feedforward*—The employee's ideas and suggestions for improvement are important. In some companies, this goes as far as sending manufacturing employees across the country to deal directly with customers.

6. *How the unit compares with others*—Employees are very interested in their own worksite and what's going on there. It's nice to get a publication once in a while about how the corporation is doing, but it's more important to know how the unit stacks up against others in the company, against the competition, and against its own previous record.

## RECOGNIZING ACHIEVEMENT

Since employees are defining their lives more and more in terms of their work, recognition for a job well done is becoming more and more important.

Data from a number of studies suggest that recognition for a job well done is the top motivation today of employee performance. Money comes in second. Money is important, especially if it is linked to how much the employee's effort aided the company, but recognition seems more important.[19] There is enough information to indicate that well-managed suggestion programs work. However, the program won't be credible if it takes too long for a suggestion to be acted on, if there is little or no monetary or personal recognition, or if results aren't significant.

## MANAGING EMPLOYEE COMMUNICATION

It has been said that this decade will be the "Decade of the Employee" for the U.S. corporation. If that is the case, people skills such as communication will be high priority.

In the early part of the decade, it appeared that the 1990s were going to be anything but the the the decade of the employee. Blue-collar jobs continued to be eliminated and work was shipped overseas. Massive downsizings among America's largest corporations ended hundreds of thousands of white-collar jobs. Those remaining employees faced bigger workloads and longer hours. They also saw more of their salary put at risk in incentive programs.

The importance of corporate communications in helping to restore and maintain credibility became apparent to more people. Key messages were aimed at explaining change, the need for attention to quality, and international competitiveness. The function of employee communication was assuming greater responsibilities, especially in an age of high-technology communications.

Respect for this function and staffing of internal communications have traditionally been meager. The median staff size for the function at the corporate level is three full-time professionals and one part-time employee.[19] CEOs apparently *now* believe more in the importance of the communications function and of its value in the future of their organization. In a Conference Board study, CEOs gave higher rankings of importance to corporate communications than to advertising or legal areas.

The statistics on corporate communications reflect some improvements: three out of four who responded to the study said they prepared an annual plan; one third had written communications policies; responsibilities in most were shared with the human resources department.[20]

Communication responsibilities included management letters and bulletins, most employee periodicals, and audio-visual productions.

Human resources responsibilities included recruitment, employee orientation, compensation, benefits, and bulletin boards. Today, the trend for internal communications will be viewed as part of human resources, not corporate communications.

The major compensation and benefits consulting firms such as Wyatt, William M. Mercer, Towers Perrin, Foster and Crosby, and the Hay Group have all maintained employee communications practices, as have the large public relations firms. This has come from a recognition that employee communication is an important part of human resources activities. The relationship between human resources and communications is more thoroughly discussed in the next chapter.

Will the function of internal communications grow? Recent surveys indicate cuts have been made in 7 out of 10 companies surveyed. Only

1 in 5 indicated any growth potential in the next few years. Service firms are more likely to have bigger staffs than manufacturers. Additional workload in over half the companies is being picked up by outside vendors. The Conference Board study went on to state that 40 percent centralize the responsibility, and less than 10 percent use a decentralized structure.

Overall, the study showed that the function has become important but continues to remain small in size. Two other factors also work to keep internal corporate communications a modest enterprise:

1. As communication responsibilities are pushed down to the line manager, corporate responsibility is reduced.
2. New communications technologies such as desktop publishing, electronic mail (e-mail), and voice messaging allow quick dissemination of information.

This is in sync with the view of the future corporate headquarters as a very small communications center with the mission of smoothing out multi-national and cultural differences. An example of the future might be seen in the move of RJR Nabisco to Atlanta—a move involving a mere 450 people into leased space in a mall.[21]

The job of internal communications in the new corporation will be two-fold: develop messages that will influence employee behavior, by focusing on *quality, productivity, morale,* and other topics important to moving the organization forward and to manage the crafting of those messages via various media, mostly through the use of free lancers and contractors. (See Table 4–1.)

In building an employee communications program, one important step is getting top-management commitment. With that commitment, a committee of senior managers needs to convene to begin the process.

Here is a seven-step method to get employee communication up and running:

1. Establish a working policy for employee communication.
2. Identify the function and staff it with professionals.
3. Recruit a steering committee to determine needs and uses.
4. Develop short- and long-range plans.
5. Use feedback to measure effectiveness.

**TABLE 4–1**
*Internal Corporate Communications*

| Old | New |
| --- | --- |
| Craftsmen | Strategists |
| Writers | Propagandists |
| Reporters | Storytellers |
| Communicators | Supporters of line |
| Makers of things | communicators |
| Part of public relations | Sellers of ideas |
| Technician | Part of human resources |
| Reactive | Designer |
| | Preemptive |

The continuum shown above demonstrates the evolution of the internal communications function in organizations. The movement is towards a more *strategic* function.

6. Budget to solve organizational problems.
7. Evaluate and revise.[22]

One of the first steps is to get supervisors to agree to some assumptions about communication:

- "Employees who understand the goals of the organization and their role in it are more likely to support those goals."
- "Supportive employees who identify with the organization are less likely to leave or be absent."
- "Employees want timely information from their supervisors."
- "Managers will do a better job if you train them."

From a strategic perspective, developing an employee communications effort should be viewed as a *marketing effort*. Employees are *consumers* of key organizational values or products—wellness, productivity, quality, customer service, safety, and so on. In establishing a communications program, the company must first conduct research to determine at what level employees are in terms of committing themselves to the organization's goals.

The question becomes, At what point do employees move from knowledge and understanding to action? Figure 4–1, a continuum developed at Communications for Management, Inc., International by Robert Nadeau

**FIGURE 4–1**

*Stages of Employee Commitment to Organization's Goals*

| Aware | Inform | Understand | Accept | Behavioral Intent | Goal-Oriented Action |
|---|---|---|---|---|---|
| Have general awareness of the issue | Up to date on issues involved | Have full knowledge of the issues and implications | Mentally accept the validity of the issue | Have decided to take action, but have not yet | Take specific action requested |

Source: Robert Nadeau, *Communications for Management*

shows the various stages of commitment employees pass through on the way to taking action:

The goal of communications is to move employees from simple awareness towards action that accomplishes the goals of the organization. Where employees are in terms of committing themselves to organizational goals will determine whether the organization can get beyond the 80/20 formula—where 20 percent of the agency's activity yields 80 percent of its results.

Such an approach requires establishing benchmarks of existing conditions and identifying the information needs of various stakeholder groups in relation to the goals of the organization. What this approach will hopefully yield is:

1. Communication needs of various employee groups.
2. Variances in commitment levels among employees.
3. Behavioral change.

## ESTABLISHING RESPONSIBILITIES

A senior management committee that has established real communications goals linked to economic performance now needs to articulate its *provable* beliefs about communications:

- That employees should understand the company's goals, the path to achieving those goals, and the employees' role in getting there.

- That there should be open and continuous communication in all directions
- That communication is a management responsibility and that managers' performance will be evaluated and rewarded based on how well they carry out these responsibilities.
- That employees are responsible for contributing ideas and suggestions to help their work units perform better.
- That information needs vary and that the communications process must provide the right information to the right people.
- That a credible process can occur only when good news and bad news are communicated.
- That employees should receive information at least concurrently with public release.

## PREPARING SUPERVISORS TO COMMUNICATE

Once the rules have been established, it is important to help managers and supervisors fulfill responsibilities including communication. Effective managers will need to be able to:

- Understand the job and demonstrate ability to translate that into daily actions.
- Provide positive and negative feedback.
- Be expert in employee communication techniques.
- Balance needs of company and people.
- Challenge people to do their best, and
- Demonstrate a capacity for exercising control over subordinates.[23]

Listening skills, team building, conflict resolution, and presentation and counseling skills will also help supervisors become good managers and communicators.

For many supervisors, leading employees is not instinctive. Those who come up the ranks are usually appointed based on their proven job skills, not their supervisory ability. Those who come from an M.B.A. program have usually received no training in supervision.[24] In these situations, *supervisors must receive training* to effectively do their jobs. In the leadership model, supervisors must also learn to become cheerleaders, who help work teams accomplish their assignments. It is estimated that as much as 70 percent of a supervisor's time is spent in verbal communication. An important part of this process is active listening, giving and receiving feedback.[25]

Better supervisory training is just one of many parts of organizational change—change that requires an overhaul of many corporate activities, procedures, and policies. The supervisor's job is particularly difficult in a time when companies are engaged in downsizings and restructurings, and when reliable information is at a premium for everyone in the organization.

Audrey Freeman of the Conference Board says that when times are tough, some bosses resort to a rigid, controlling management style. They are threatened by more open systems. She adds that companies facing cutbacks naturally drift towards a more open style, not because they think it is right, but because that is what allows them to take greatest advantage of the worker's skills.[26]

## MANAGING COMMUNICATIONS PERFORMANCE

Supervisors/managers often need to be prodded to communicate. The only effective technique is to make communications a major accountability in performance measurement and link accomplishments to salary increases, incentives, and promotions. The term is a familiar one—*pay for performance*.

### Conflicting Evidence

Two items:

- In the late 1980s, General Motors went to extraordinary lengths to make its entire management/supervisory staff more involved in employee communications. The focus of a major initiative was to sell managers on two-way communications, keep employees informed, and make communications more open. This effort involved print, media, and a special training seminar.[27] In 1991, the company experienced record *losses* and initiated a major restructuring with an anticipated loss of 72,000 jobs.

- A union worker at Caterpillar, reflecting on a long lockout during early 1992, said, "They (management) tell you how important you are to their success and then they go out and try and break the union when we represent only 6–12% of their costs."[28]

## *Upward Communications*

Like any good marketer selling a product, managers selling the company's vision to employees need good research to tell them if their efforts are working. But employee feedback provides even greater value when employees are not only willing to talk about themselves but are willing to give ideas that will help improve organizational performance. IBM's *Speak Up!* program, for example, has resulted in 400,000 questions and concerns from employees in the 32 years since it began.

The question always arises: Should an upwards communications program be anonymous? The answer is complex. In a more traditional company, yes. In a more advanced, evolving organization, frank and candid comments from identifiable employees will be valued. The larger the organization, the more difficult it is to accomplish upward communication, or feedforward. There are dozens of ideas that have been suggested over the years. Here are a few:

1. Systems for listening via first line supervisors.
   a. Personal interviews.
   b. Face-to-face meetings with small groups.
2. Unit systems.
   a. Suggestion programs.
   b. Search out 10 people in the unit. Arm yourself with a set of questions and go get the answers.
3. Corporate systems.
   a. Encourage and print candid letters in the employee publication.
   b. Publication readership surveys.
   c. Formal attitude surveys.

Also providing financial incentives and recognition have long been recognized as an effective means of encouraging employee feedback.

## EMPLOYEE COMMUNICATIONS PLANNING

The old saw is "give them what we think they need to know." A better approach might be to give them what they need to create value for the company.

If this is the starting point, the first step is to gather information from:

- *Current business issues*—What issues is the organization currently facing? Is the company expanding? Downsizing? What are the competitive demands on employees?
- *Top management*—What opportunities/challenges do they see? What are their goals? Key issues?
- *Written materials*—The annual report, business plan, research reports.
- *Company departments*—Visit each part of the company and talk with employees at all levels. Do they share the same information? Values? How do they get information about what's going on? How much do they understand about what is going on?
- *Trade associations and publications*—What are the trends for the business? What does the business press say about your industry? Your business? The outlook?

What do employees need to know to create value? There may be variances between what management thinks they know and what employees really know. Information sent down often bottlenecks at the managerial level.

Employees have two sets of information needs.[30] One need is business information: what's going on at their own specific location. They need to understand where the organization is going, how management is going to get there, and what the employees' role is in that process. More than just knowing this, however, they need to commit themselves to it.

The second kind of information they need is personal information: compensation/benefits/performance appraisal, recognition, development, and promotions. These information needs are more immediately important to them, and need to be satisfied before they are willing to listen to management's problems. Evaluation of these individual needs can be accomplished through a number of ways, including a good upward communication system that allows employees the opportunity not only to affect the decision-making process but also to ask questions and get answers.

Methods that encourage *upward* communication include surveys, polls, interactive systems (such as voice response or computer feedback), hotlines, and suggestion systems.

Once information is available, management can determine where employees are in relation to each organizational goal on a continuum ranging from simple awareness to goal-oriented action (see Figure 4–1). Goal-oriented action is behaviorally based and demonstrated via specific actions such as productivity and quality improvements. Once that determination is made, management can establish objectives and develop an action plan. For example, if we want to cut employee benefit costs by 10 percent, do we give them more information on benefit programs so they will make wiser decisions, or do we introduce a wellness program? The evaluation will tell us.

## ESTABLISHING A VALUE CREATION STRATEGY

The value creation model, shown in Figure 4–2, starts with specifying *desired outcomes* that are linked to the organization's goals: for example, reduce product defects to 2 per 100,000. Next, *data collection* tells us that 120 employees are involved in production and none are on incentive. In the next step, *benchmarking*, we learn that the present defect rate is 12 per 100,000. After brainstorming, we *develop a strategy* of dividing the group into work teams and instituting an incentive program. We put together our communication *tactics*, which include a group meeting to announce the program and team briefings by supervisors. *Implementation* goes on schedule and *measurement* takes place two months later to observe progress and establish corrections, if needed.

### What Can Managers Start Doing Today?

Some suggestions for immediate improvement in employee communication include:

1. *Increase management-employee contact and communication.* The best way to go about this is to create opportunities, formally, through increased meetings and feedback sessions, but also informally, through organization of building and office space, and lunch rooms to get management out of the office. Staff visits to the shop floor and office areas build credibility, boost morale, and show management visibly involved at the local level. Does this sound like a political campaign? It is.

Even more radical is the idea, espoused by Westinghouse, to ask plant staff to take turns in the shop working on various hourly jobs.

Other approaches include brown bag lunches, in which staff meets informally with employees to tell them what's going on and to answer questions. In larger organizations, skip-level lunches, in which top man-

**FIGURE 4–2**
*The Value Creation Model*

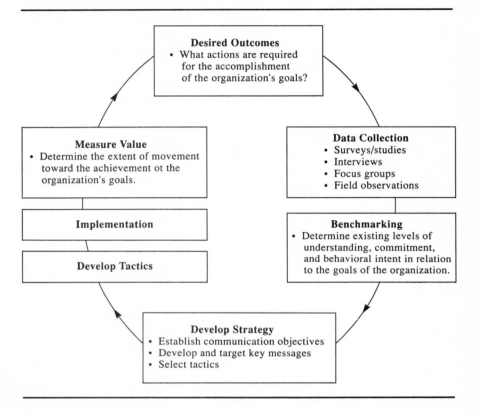

agement meets with lower level managers, helps keep senior managers on their toes and gives top management the chance to see if communications is really going up and down the line.

2. *Make supervisors/managers accountable for relaying information.* Systems that force managers to document their delivery of information to employees can be installed. Another technique includes a reverse evaluation system, in which employees rate their managers on a number of factors, including communications.

3. *Develop channels that get information to supervisors and managers quickly.* With today's high-speed telecommunications and information systems, getting information to all levels of management is simple and

efficient. Companies everywhere are utilizing computer e-mail and voice mail to quickly get the word out to supervisors.

4. *Tell employees how their unit is doing compared to other units and the company as a whole*. This is a job managers can do face-to-face. And most employees care more about this than they do about the four-color magazine mailed home about corporate events.

5. *Expand upward communications*. There are no easy ways to do this. Suggestion programs that provide both recognition and monetary reward have produced annual savings of millions of dollars to companies that support them through aggressive communications. Regular employee attitude surveys provide a pictures of where employees are.

### New Initiatives, New Times

Communication campaigns can be designed today at the corporate level and left to line management to implement. In one project the author was involved in for a major Midwestern company, the assignment was to develop an aggressive information campaign to inform manufacturing employees around the country about a new incentive program that would replace a traditional year-end bonus.

Working with management, we developed a strategy to train plant managers and personnel directors at the plants in the program, provide them with an easy-to-understand print piece, and have them explain the program to employees. In order to force increased management-employee communication we limited support to overhead slides. The program was planned to make managers the key resource on how the program would work and to force them to "stand and deliver" the information and rationale to employees.

Corporate communications can develop, and has, over the years, developed many successful programs in a great number of areas—recycling, energy saving, accident prevention, substance abuse, quality programs, and so on.

In recent years, employee relations has matured from the stereotypical newsletter filled with birth announcements, gold watch presentations, and bowling scores. Today's employees have more sophisticated interests. They are more diverse and multicultural and they have media savvy. The company newsletter gives old-time managers a warm feeling of control, but does nothing for moving the organization forward. The old message of "one big happy family" does not work in an environment where continuous layoffs and downsizings, strikes, continuous management shifts, reorganizations, and bad press are often the reality.

## The Outside-In Theory

Today's employees are media-sensitive and sophisticated about issues like inflation, recession, interest rates, and world trade. "If they see a story on television about fraud or corruption [in their company], they look to the [company's media] to deny that information," said one corporate communications director. She called it the "outside-in" theory: If employees see a story in the media they look to company people or media to confirm or deny it and vice versa. One insurance company, attacked in the media for alleged red-lining practices in the community, found itself with a big employee morale problem. The communications department, through its in-house television service, televised top executives who rebutted the attack. People want to say, "I still work for a good company."[31]

## New Technologies for New Employees

In the last decade, companies began adding new technologies to improve communication—voice messaging, networked computer systems, video networks, tele/video conferencing systems between locations, and desktop publications, to name the most common.

The new systems provide greater interconnectability between departments and units, and allow publications to be quickly produced in-house and targeted to different audiences.

Nevertheless, the bread and butter of employee communications is still the print medium. The trend in print has been towards less glitz and more relevant content. Articles covering the changing nature of the company's business, key customers, product information, and international concerns have replaced the more traditional human interest copy.

## Today's Employee Publication

For an example of today's new employee magazine, look at the spring 1988 issue of *The Corner Stone*, Stone Container Corporation's quarterly magazine, which was mailed to company employees' homes. Stories included an industry outlook, which noted that the company was doing better generally than the industry at the time. Other articles discussed:

- The job of wood procurement for the company's 10 virgin fiber mills.
- Stone's newest acquisition.
- The restart of a failed plant in Florida.
- The entry of the company into two new markets: newsprint and market pulp.
- How the company uses recycled materials.
- Cogeneration at the company's mills.
- Federal environmental legislation.

Also included was a page of covered statistics, a quiz on company history, some facts on AIDS, point-of-purchase products using Stone cardboard, brief executive profiles, and a page of grateful letters from employees—every company employee had been given a color TV set because of record sales.[32]

Videos today are considered an adjunct to print. Half the companies in the Conference Board poll cited earlier said they used video for boosting morale, promoting goodwill, supplying information about company products, encouraging employees to be more productive, and updating them on salary and benefits.[33]

## SUMMARY

Soldiers with good morale are better fighters. And soldiers don't go into battle without understanding the objective, the goal, and the reason for the battle. Employees who know the game plan, understand the reasons and what the rewards will be will also be victors, if they are well led. Maybe that old military model still fits.

## ENDNOTES

1. Peter Drucker, *Managing for Results* (New York: Harper & Row, 1986), pp.45–46.
2. Mark Frohman, "American Organizations: Right Aim, Bad Implementation," *Industry Week*, December 2, 1991, pp. 12–18.
3. Communications consultants and researchers have long labored to establish direct linkage between communications and profitability. Research under-

taken at Communications for Management, Inc. International by Robert Nadeau, a consultant and graduate researcher in organizational communications at Loyola University in Chicago, turned up a model we believe makes a strong case for the value creation power of communication.

4. David W. Ewing, "Practical Incentives for Helping Employeys Make Themselves Heard," *Management Review*, January 1983, pp. 14–17.

5. Hay Management Consultants, "Business Culture and Performance," Presentation, Chicago, Ill. 1982.

6. Robert A. Judd, "Employee Communication Targets a Changing Audience," *Communication World*, July 1984, p. 51.

7. Ronald Goodman and Richard S. Ruch, "In the Image of the CEO," *Public Relations Journal*, February 1981, pp. 14–19.

8. Hank Bachrach, "It's Deja Vu All Over Again or Let's Not Reinvent the Wheel Unless . . ." *IABC Communication World*, January 1992, pp. 21–24.

9. Noel L.Griese, "The Employee Communication Philosophy of Arthur W. Page," *Public Relations Quarterly*, Winter 1977, pp. 8–12.

10. Julie Foehrenbach and Steve Foldfarb, "Employee Communication in the '90s Great(er) Expectations, *Communication World*, May/June 1990, pp. 101–106. Conclusions were derived from a database of Towers, Perrin, Foster, and Crosby in about 300 organizations in the period 1987–1989.

11. Stephen Franklin, "Workers Say Bosses Neither Lend nor Bend an Ear," *Chicago Tribune*, March 27, 1992, p. 3-1.

12. Cathy Klepack, "Effective Communications Leads to Higher Profits, *Bank Marketing*, September 1990, pp. 33–35.

13. Roger D'Aprix, *Communicating for Productivity* (New York: Harper & Row Publishers, 1982), p. 12.

14. Valorie McClelland, "Employees We Trust," *Personnel Administrator*, September 1988, pp. 137–139.

15. Franklin, "Workers Say Bosses Neither Lend nor Bend an Ear," p. 3–1.

16. Internal company report, "Communicating for Productivity," The Weyerhauser Company, May 1982.

17. D'Aprix, *Communicating for Productivity*, p. 19

18. Peggy Stuart, "Fresh Ideas Energize Reward Programs," *Personnel Journal*, January 1992, p. 102.

19. Kathryn Troy, "Internal Communication Restructures for the '90s," *Communication World*, February 1989, pp. 28–31.

20. Elaine Goldman and Joseph Coppolino, "CEOs view PR issues in '89," *Communication World*, January 1989, pp. 28–31.

21. Robert L. Dilenschneider, "Merging Turf: Why Communications and Business Consulting Are Converging," *IABC Communication World*, January 1992, pp. 48–49.

22. Chuck Slocum, "Employee Communication Is More Than Sharing Information with Employees, *Journal of Organizational Communication*, Fall 1981, pp 6–8.

23. James Lomac and Thomas Rand, "All Managers Are Not Created Equal," *Data Management*, November 1983, pp. 30–31.

24. Elizabeth M. Fowler, "Special Training for M.B.A.'s," *New York Times*, February 17, 1992, p. C17.

25. Delbert W. Fisher, "A Model for Better Communication," *Supervisory Management*, June 1982, pp. 24–29.

26. Bruce H. Goodsite, "General Motors Attacks Its Frozen Middle," *Communication World*, October 1987, pp. 20–23.

27. Douglas C. Curley, "The Other Half of Employee Communication," *Personnel Administrator*, July 1979, pp. 28–32.

28. Franklin, "Workers Say Bosses Neither Lend nor Bend an Ear," p. 3–1.

29. "All Things Considered," Report on Caterpillar strike, NPR Newscast, February 19, 1992.

30. Valorie McClelland, "Developing an Employee Communication Plan," *Personnel Management: Communications*, (Englewood-Cliffs, New Jersey, 1989), pp. 1565–1569.

31. Interview with Nan Kilkearry, Allstate Insurance Company, quoted in Frank M. Corrado, *Media for Managers*, Englewood Cliffs, New Jersey: Prentice-Hall, 1984, pp. 113–14.

32. *The Corner Stone*, no. 2 (Spring 1988).

33. Troy, "Internal Communication Restructures for the '90s," pp. 28–31.

# Chapter Five

# Human Resources Communication

The successful deployment of human resources will be America's edge in the world market. As managements realize that people are the only nonexportable factor of production, they will begin to invest more in developing those resources.

When Chrysler opened its new $1.2 billion Jefferson Avenue North plant in innercity Detroit in 1992, each of its 2,500 workers had received an average of 500 hours of training to prepare them for a self-directed team approach to manufacturing. Average age of the workers was 51 years old with 26 years of seniority. The building of the plant was meant to counter Japanese claims that U.S. workers were lazy and uneducated, and to show that a U.S. company can fulfill moral obligations to workers and the community.[1]

A wide range of human resources initiatives in the past decade show that management is attempting to do more to develop human resources through quality circles, pay for performance, expanded training, employee assistance and motivation. Today's hot buttons include developing the multicultural workforce, employee empowerment, organizational development, and flexible benefits.

As a result, human resources is emerging as the new home of internal communications in many companies. Driving this is management's need for help with the strategic alignment of the work force to new marketplace realities.

But while management has begun to embrace greater employee involvement and empowerment, the longstanding contract of "loyalty for job security" between employer and employee has dissolved, and the result is a strained relationship. As a result, a new era of worker confrontation appears to be looming.

Through 1995, one in five companies is expected to downsize or restructure each year. Thirty-seven percent of the 1979 Fortune 500 companies no longer existed in 1992, and 50 percent of the 1979 Fortune 500 retailers have totally disappeared. As many as 58 percent of the transportation companies are gone. And 10 industries in the 1980s saw 40 percent of their members disappear. Since 1985, the number of major corporations with no-layoff policies dropped from 30 to 7.[2]

Management's view of communication in this new era is that communication must improve, not because good employee communication is nice to have, but because communication is part of the strategic plan designed to create measurable value for the organization.

An organization's human resource strategy links the economic mission of the organization to the organization and deployment of its people.

The mission of human resource strategy has traditionally included five activities:

1. Organizational design and development—The process of clarifying and documenting jobs and reporting structures, job specifications, and interrelationships.

2. Staffing and continuity—Getting the best people to fill positions and making sure there are more positions and people available as needs arise.

3. Performance management—Motivating and developing people to make effective contributions towards the organization's and their own personal well-being.

4. Administration and compliance—Managing the allocation of compensation dollars to achieve maximum results, and adhering to regulatory guidelines.

5. Welfare—Providing the services that contribute to the health and well-being of individuals and employee groups.[3]

Today, organizations are making a number of strategic human resource changes—reducing benefits, restructuring and downsizing, putting more compensation at risk, linking rewards more closely to performance, and providing increased training and employee assistance. The trend has been to reduce personnel costs as much as possible without losing the ability to attract and retain good employees.

In these attempts to make the organization more competitive, management is coming more and more to the human resources director for help in getting employees' commitment to the mission, vision, and values of the organization. This strategic role is new to human relations, and it has become increasingly obvious that linkages must be developed with the communications function of the organization. Because of the strategic role that human relations now plays—the more craft-oriented services provided by the communications function—human relations now is more involved in directing the internal use of communication.

The interface between communication and human resources runs throughout a long list of accountabilities that include:

1. Performance Management.
   a. Mission/vision/values.
   b. Performance appraisal.
   c. Training and development.
   d. EAP.
   e. Employee relations.
2. Personnel.
   a. Recruiting.
   b. Compensation.
   c. Benefits.
   d. Orientation.
3. Welfare.
   a. Affirmative action.
   b. Retirement planning.
   c. Employee rights.
   d. Charitable contributions
3. Administration.
   a. Personnel policies and procedures.
   b. Salary administration.
   c. Employee records.
4. Continuity.
   a. Career planning.
   b. Succession planning.
   c. Staffing planning.
5. Compliance.
   a. Monitoring.
   b. Complaints.
   c. Influence.
   d. FLSA.
   e. NLRA.
   f. EEO.
   g. OSHA.
   h. ADA.

## BUILDING LINKAGES

An organizational strategy to bring communications and human resources together will need to include these steps:

- Get management commitment to strengthened human resources communications.
- Develop a human resource policy statement on communication.
- Assign responsibilities between communications and human resources.
- Allocate resources.

Specific steps for *human resources* will be to:

- Identify communication priorities.
- Establish capabilities and assign responsibilities.
- Develop and implement a program linked to organizational goals.

Specific human resources strategy for the *communications* department will include:

- Benchmark employee concerns via attitude survey.
- Develop specific program activities with human resources.
- Produce tactical materials and execute programs.
- Evaluate results for linkage to corporate objectives.

Today, as the CEO is becoming more focused on organizational issues, the human resources director is being given more strategic responsibilities for strategic planning. But strategic implementation is becoming more decentralized, down to the supervisory level in today's flattened organization. A new substance abuse program, for example, may be developed at the corporate level, but the plant employee relations manager or the plant manager must communicate it, answer questions about it, and make sure it is implemented. Companies are training managers at all levels of the organization to be more involved in the delivery of human resources services.

In an environment where employees want to hear information from their supervisors, internal communications people must produce materials that the supervisor can use for a targeted work audience—production workers, office staff, other managers, unionized labor, and so on.

But giving managers information to communicate to employees is only part of the process—those managers must understand how important this is to their job. They must receive training in interpersonal communication, and their financial reward must be at least partially based on how well they communicate with their employees. Only then will a decentralized system work.

The development of appropriate communication materials must be a joint exercise between human resources and communications that results in messages that are clearly matched to specific corporate human resources objectives, delivered according to a specific timetable, and evaluated in terms of measurable behavior change. Generally speaking, human resources managers do not possess the skills for developing and implementing communication programs, so they must either hire those skills via outside consultants and vendors or assume greater management of the internal (management communications) activities.

The communications person can bring to the table a better sense of what can and cannot be communicated to employees and how best to do it. Human resources managers, from the old days of labor relations, tend to be more reluctant to give out information, whereas communication people, with their traditional journalistic perspective, tend to promote more open communication.

The urgency and need for realigning the work force is crucial. The marriage between communication and human resources is a done deal.

## SPECIAL HUMAN RESOURCES COMMUNICATION PROBLEMS

The impacts of restructuring, rising benefits costs, compensation, and performance management have provided major communication challenges to the organization. Below are communication strategies for handling these specific issues.

### *Communicating with Survivors*

Companies involved in mergers will have significant communication problems, mostly because there is so much energy focused on putting the deal together and executing the merger that things like communicating to employees seem to get lost in the shuffle. By identifying communication up front as a major issue and identifying responsible officials in both managements to work as a team on the problem will reduce some of the consequences.

Companies engaged in these activities say that the biggest problem is finding time to communicate via face-to-face and staff meetings.[4]

When companies cut back their work forces, most of the care and concern is directed towards those who are leaving. But what about those who remain? Current research shows a number of negative downsizing impacts: decreased productivity, substandard performance, job dissatisfaction, low worker involvement, lost loyalty, and increased conflict.

Goals need to be established for employees that will:

- Help them understand the grieving process.
- Get them to communicate feelings.
- Develop strong team skills.
- Counteract negative communications.
- Develop a positive approach.
- Set goals and plans in the new work environment.

### For supervisors: "Put on Your Oxygen Mask First"

Many times, managers suffer the most in a downsizing. They not only have to deal with the issues of loss encountered by their employees, but oftentimes harbor anger and guilt over having to be the one to carry out a directed layoff. It's important that they acknowledge to someone how they feel.

Cutbacks pose significant psychological problems, but these problems are magnified in leadership roles. Rebuilding a company is not an event— it is a process. If it is not viewed that way, people may leave, or worse, they may stay on and not be part of the rebuilding.

People in work groups go through predictable states when a downsizing occurs: denial, anger, recovery. Supervisors can't hide in their offices; they need to talk with employees and help them with their jobs. Supervisors also need to be concerned for their own mental health. They need to watch the stress level, try to be around people who are positive and supportive, and not harbor negative feelings.

### Saying Goodbye to the Past

Farewell rituals, announcements, meetings, and the like, help people feel their way through the situation in a safe manner. Survivor guilt can be dealt with by letting employees help those who are being terminated. Employees must be told what is being done for those terminated, and it is crucial to deal head-on with the constant rumors that circulate. Here's how to do it:

- Establish a pipeline to get into the rumor loop.
- Confront rumors with facts.
- Move quickly to confirm or deny rumors.
- Make sure there's a way for employees to get information on rumors.

### Helping Survivors

You have to pay a lot of attention to survivors, including increasing in-house training and development, and helping employees redesign their jobs. Remember that people who thrived in the old environment may be poor performers in the new work culture. Creativity, for example, may now be more valued than in the old environment. You need to work with your people on developing the skills that are important in the new environment. Developing a staff for the future flies in the face of the emphasis for a quick turnaround.

A nine-step process for helping survivors has been developed and successfully used:[5]

1. *Self-assessment*—Honest self-appraisal of the individual's emotional response to this difficult situation is a first step. It should be aided by the supervisor.

2. *Managing the grief process*—There needs to be open discussion and sharing of feelings of confusion and distress. Hold an "Irish wake" for those who have gone. Acknowledge the loss of them and the past. Don't try to pretend it never happened.

3. *Goal-setting*—Goals must be short and long term. Optimally, they should be set with the employees, rather than from the top down. Everyone needs to share in putting together the turnaround process. They have to be focused beyond the downsizing phase with milestones and benchmarks for progress.

4. *Plan with your people*—Involve them in the process. Work with them to figure out how to do Mary's and John's work, now that they are no longer there.

5. *Communicate expectations*—Explain what the new job requirements are going to be in positive terms. Listen and they will be more receptive.

6. *Provide a growth environment*—Employees are now going to have to begin solving problems more on their own. Supervisors have to recognize this and give them latitude in coming up with their own ideas.

7. *Monitor performance*—Increase performance measurement to make sure the new process is working.

8. Feedback—This must be done both in terms of team and individual performance. Team performance keeps the big picture in mind. Having survived the downsizing, team members will have a group cohesiveness strengthened by having shared a common experience.

9. *Empower your employees*—Employees need ways of gaining confidence and working through their feelings if they are going to invest emotional energies in their jobs. You need to know your people and what particular incentives motivate them. For some, it will be group awards, a bonus, more pay, or recognition. Use group pressure. You need to increase employee relations activities also—wellness, vision meetings, and so forth.

## *If Cutbacks Are Still Pending. . .*

Work groups will often divide between those leaving and those staying. In this situation, a great amount of animosity and hostility is often present. Those leaving are resentful over the loss of their jobs and often project their anger at those remaining. Those staying on are often uncomfortable and may even feel guilty.

One technique for dealing with this problem is to organize efforts by those remaining to share networks, contacts, and other information that will be helpful to those looking for a new job. Also, try to remember that it is normal for people to be sad, angry, giddy, and highstrung, all within the same day. Powerful emotions tend to do that to people.

Don't treat those leaving as if they were lepers. They're the same people they were yesterday. You will be judged by those who remain by the way you treat those who are leaving.

Here are some important points for managers to keep in mind:

1. Set personal goals. Victims don't set goals; they only react. A proactive stance will speed recovery.

2. Recognize achievement. Recognize positive aspects to negative events. Time is necessary to heal the psychological pain, and management must be hopeful, honest, and liberal with its use of praise and positive statements. This is the time to manage with soft hands and gentleness.

## *Communicating Compensation in the 1990s*

A major method for motivating employees is to design reward systems that spur employees to greater performance thus creating more value for the company.

One approach companies have been emphasizing is the philosophy of pay for performance. But some companies espousing this approach continue merit pay increases which undermine the pay for performance approach. Total quality program adherents believe that market rate, gain sharing and seniority should be key compensation criteria. Performance-based pay plans linked to quality and productivity rather than profits are producing results, especially for non-management employees.

New strategies emphasize putting more and more compensation at risk as an inducement to greater performance. For salaried employees, the move is to individual plans linking annual increases to achievement of measurable, written objectives. For hourly or nonexempt employees, new plans base a percentage of compensation on team performance against established goals. Other new compensation models include lump-sum, or one-time payments that are performance-based bonuses and do not become part of base compensation.

With these pay philosophy changes, compensation communications is more important than ever. Employees rank compensation communications as one of the key areas of information needs. As companies move toward more performance-based systems, employees need to understand what the rules are and how they can compete for additional dollars.

The new pay strategies require that managers become key interpreters of compensation plans, since it is those same managers who will be required, in many cases, to establish performance criteria, and evaluate accomplishment of objectives.

Here is a typical sequence:

**Establish communications goals.** Some examples of goals here include:

- Provide a timely announcement of the new program or modifications to those impacted.
- Interpret and emphasize the value of the salary administration program.
- Answer immediate questions that participants may have.
- Motivate employees by gaining their support for fair and equitable administration of the salary program.
- Promote better employee-management relations.
- Increase employee morale and productivity.
- Give managers and supervisors knowledge and skills to implement the program.
- Provide continuing communications about pay and performance.
- Demonstrate the relationship of pay, benefits, and job environment as parts of total compensation.
- Offer employees the opportunity to give feedback about their questions, concerns, perceptions, and attitudes concerning the organization's pay program.

**Identify subject areas for communication.** The subject areas might include:

- Why a new program or why changes are being made.
- Objectives of the new program.
- How job evaluation is conducted.
- How the program provides internal equity—fairness for all.
- What the company's pay philosophy is, whether to pay at market rates, or to be the top payer.
- External competitiveness of the program.
- Linkage to performance.

**Identify audience targets and needs.** There are a number of audiences to consider:

- Top management—Provide them with sufficient information to gain commitment and support to make policy decisions. Get their top assistants on the job evaluation committee.

- Salary administrators—Make them knowledgeable in the detailed operation of the program.
- Supervisors—Require detailed information to be able to answer employee questions and make salary recommendations.
- Employees—Provide them with an overview of the program. They need to know their performance will be rewarded, and that the program is fair and competitive.
- Special audiences—The sales force and managers must understand the relationship between base compensation and incentives, short term and long term. Potential employees need to know the key features of the plan: fairness, equity, competitiveness, and pay for performance.

**Conduct research on needs.**   Try to find out what employees already know. Determine how much misinformation they have received and what their general feelings and perceptions are. In addition, determine the audience level including their educational background, so that you will know how much detailed information needs to be given.

**Select media.**   Selection of appropriate media depends on your audience profile, how many locations are involved, the organizational style, budget concerns, and whether the communication will be reused later on during orientation.

Types of media include:

- Letters or memos (best for announcement of program).
- Articles in employee publications (best for updates on the program's progress). Key points to stress include representation from all parts of the company in the process.
- Employee meetings utilizing audiovisual and question-and-answer session.
- A visually oriented program works best: video or slides, with a take-away brochure graphically showing the entire process. The brochure should also feature a message from the CEO, a diagram of the pay evaluation program, and the most commonly asked questions and their answers. The communication should stress why the company is changing its program, and emphasize key attributes.
- Highlight folders.
- Payroll stuffers.

- Telephone hotline or tape message system.
- Poster and bulletin boards.
- Employee handbooks.

**Establish a timetable.**   Make sure your communications plan is linked to milestones—beginning with the start of the evaluation process and concluding with a major communications effort during roll-out. This period can run as long as six months to a year.

**Train and link to other programs.**   Compensation programs should not be communicated in a vacuum. Benefits are part of total compensation, and performance evaluation is closely linked to compensation. These linkages must be communicated to employees. The best way to communicate this information is via supervisors in these subject areas.

### Benefits Communication

Benefits communication can motivate employees to get more involved in choosing new options that match their needs and  save their organization money.

Benefits communication has become a priority today as:

1. Companies install new flexible-benefit programs that give employees the opportunity to get involved in designing individualized programs.
2. Companies seek to provide more cost-effective benefits in the face of rising health-care costs, often through new cost-sharing arrangements with employees.
3. Government tax policy on benefits continues to change and legislation becomes more complex.
4. The population of the United States ages. Retirement planning is particularly complex because of new legislation, longer life spans, and rising health-care costs for covered retirees.

**Great expectations—employer and employee.**   *Employers* need to communicate both value and scope of new benefits programs. They need to make sure employees understand the additional value that benefits provide in total compensation (as much as 20 percent to 40 percent). Also, communication can point employees toward using their benefits more wisely. Providing extra time for implementing and communicating can pay off in better decisions.

*Employees* expect benefits communication to clearly and simply spell out what they are getting and what their choices are. Because employee groups have such diverse backgrounds, information needs to be presented in alternative formats.

## Key Elements of a Communications Plan

Studies show employees fail to read written benefits material that is only minimally communicated. This can cost both the employee and the company money when bad choices follow.

Here is a step-by-step approach for developing a benefits communications plan:

1. Research—Should the communications be low key or glitzy? Should it be high-tech interactive software or just a handout? The best way to find out is to ask employees, via focus groups, how they would like to get their information. If a company has been going through hard times, it makes sense to be low key. The real reason for glitzy communications is that it gets through to people.

2. Strategy—The most important step in the whole process is determining audiences and messages. While all employees may be covered under the plan, a good communications strategy recognizes that there are a number of employee subgroups—new hire, mid-career, near retirement—with different needs. Today's benefits are designed with the needs of these subgroups in mind, and the accompanying communications must address them.

Include a timeline for implementation. Budgets for communication can vary greatly, but a reasonable minimum is about 10 percent of the total cost.

Benefits program changes, such as increasing employee health-care contributions, should be explained in the wider context of what is happening in society as a whole. In sum, a program must not only inform, but also motivate employees to take action.

3. Hand-out materials—Materials that include descriptions, benefit statements, worksheets, and enrollment and beneficiary forms can be presented to employees in a folder.

4. Scheduled presentations—These are ideal for small groups and should be conducted whenever major changes are made. Small groups

allow for questions and answers. Large groups are more efficient but can add to downtime costs and may require supplemental question-and-answer materials or forums. For large and/or dispersed organizations, new technologies can be substituted, but they remove the people-to-people factor.

5. Visually based communications—These should be part of any presentation because today's employees are video watchers. The problem with many benefits videos and slide shows is that they look like they were produced by a tax accountant.

Calculations and complex explanations should be saved for print. The power of the visual medium is to use real-life examples to demonstrate concepts. Keep visual communications simple. Stick with highlights. Use diagrams and easy-to-understand flow charts and graphics.

6. Coordinated print pieces—These should accompany any visual presentation. A take-away print piece reminds the employee of the highlights of the presentation.

7. Interactive computer programs are now available. The overall goal is to help deal with individual questions concerning a complex program.

8. Evaluation will tell you if the program worked. Simple mail-back cards with questions designed to test the effectiveness of the communications effort will help ensure that the program worked.

Communications tools to choose from include:

• *Generic packages*. A number of insurance and benefit consulting firms have developed generic communications and enrollment packages that can be adapted for budget-minded companies.

• *Television*. Videos are very good at delivering an impression, a feeling, about the program. A video can also serve to point out highlights and deliver the company's message on wise benefit use. Many businesses use take-offs on popular TV shows to get the point across. The MTV generation expects a snappy look.

• *Interactive computer software*. One of the most advanced is at Levi Strauss & Co., which has instituted OLIVER, the on-line interactive visual employee resource, where each employee can access the main frame and look not only at benefits but also at such areas as financial planning, training, and development.[6]

• *Automated voice response*. This technology allows users to enter their selections via voice mail after they've read materials sent via mail.

• *Print*. Even on computer disk, you're still reading words. Print is the oldest and most basic communication tool of benefits communication.

Today, it's seen as a supplement to more advanced communications technologies, but in a pinch, it works fine by itself, especially with interactive pieces like worksheets.

• *Meetings.* Most employees still prefer to get information on a one-on-one basis from supervisors. Small and large group meetings don't rank as high, but do work when a strong graphic element is present, like a video or slides.

• *Slides/overheads.* These are the traditional methods for presenting benefits information in meetings. Although slides and overheads are not high tech, they allow the presenter to interject him- or herself into presentation. In the past, too many of these shows have tended to look like financial statements.

• *Videoconferences.* These are evangelical in nature, bringing together the corporate faithful by satellite, nationwide or worldwide, to hear about the new program and what it means. This is a good technique for waving the flag on benefits.

• *Hotlines.* For medium-to-large organizations, this is an important tool for employees to have access to in order to get very specific answers to their questions. The problem is that hotlines need to be staffed adequately by knowledgeable specialists.

• *Payroll processing systems.* Information on benefits is directly communicated to employees via each payroll statement, so that employees know what their benefits are at all times. This information cuts down on questions.

Special communications activities cover plan enrollment marketing, communicating wellness, and decreasing workman's compensation payouts. Planning enrollment marketing for 401(k) programs, among others, requires a vote by employees before the program can be adopted. Communication campaigns for this effort should follow all the rules of marketing—emphasizing product, placement, promotion, and pricing.

Communicating wellness—fitness, nutrition, managing stress, and quitting smoking—can make a difference. General publications and customized periodicals are available for small and medium companies.

The best communications strategy for cutting high workers' compensation costs includes attacking these subjects: (1) avoiding injuries, (2) managing healthcare costs, and (3) preventing suits. This requires promoting workplace safety, promoting fitness and a positive mental attitude, and developing and implementing an ergonomic approach to the job.

## *Communicating Job Performance*

Helping establish an environment where people perform at their best is a major responsibility of human resources. Performance management is a skill that must be imparted to managers and supervisors.

Performance evaluation systems must:

- Give employees the opportunity to participate in the planning and reviewing of their performance.
- Promote understanding of how the goals of the job relate to the overall goals of the unit and to the organization in general.
- Help determine financial recognition based on achievement. They must be linked clearly to established, quantifiable objectives.

The new emphasis in performance evaluation is to:

- Retain and motivate top performers.
- More closely link pay and performance.
- Recognize individual performance to a greater degree.
- Increase employee participation in setting goals.
- Establish individual growth and development plans.
- Link job responsibilities with organizational values.

Performance communication must be conducted at two levels:

1. *Organizationwide*. New programs need to be communicated companywide to both supervisors and employees. Supervisors need to understand how the program works and be given interpersonal skills to implement it. Employees as a group need to understand changes in the program and how they will be evaluated.

2. *One-on-one between manager/supervisor and employee* Managers/supervisors must be trained in interpersonal communications skills to effectively conduct performance appraisals.

Each phase of the performance management process has communication components:

1. Planning—Supervisor and employee meet to establish measurable objectives for the coming year.
2. Performance management—Management monitors performance on a continuing basis and conducts progress reviews.
3. Formal evaluation—At the close of the performance period, manager and employee review the manager's written evaluation and discuss ratings and salary impact.

4. Planning for future development—The manager/supervisor discusses future possibilities with the employee. They agree upon a plan to help with areas that need improvement and review and adjust the development objectives for the coming year.

Employees rank communications as one of the key areas of information needs. As companies move toward more performance-based systems, it is important that employees understand what the rules are and how they can compete for additional dollars.

As companies throughout the United States move toward total quality management (TQM) systems, they are beginning to wrestle with a key tenet of TQM: performance appraisal programs don't work. The timing is ironic, since most companies have just begun to accept the idea of pay for performance.

The TQM argument is that individual performance is difficult to measure and results in competition among employees. Studies show that almost all companies that get into TQM make at least some changes to their performance management systems.

TQM stresses the importance of the team over the individual, the need to measure behavior more quantitatively, and the concept of utilizing short-term incentives and minimizing merit increases. Other TQM strategies include both peer and customer feedback. All of this hacks at the concept of individual reward and management review of performance.

Others argue that an organization's culture should drive performance measurement, especially since the tradition of many American companies is to encourage individualism. But the momentum is toward new systems that foster collaboration and teamwork.

The new systems tie compensation to an employee's seniority, level of expertise, and the overall market for his or her services. Most companies, however, probably won't get rid of their performance appraisal systems soon. Changing cultures and educating employees will take a long time. Inroads, however, are being made in terms of pay for performance programs that are putting more compensation at risk.

For salaried employees, individual plans are showing more linkage of annual increases to achievement of measurable, written objectives. For hourly or nonexempt employees, new plans are basing a percentage of compensation on team performance against established goals, rather than on seniority.

## Communications and Unions

Research has shown that companies strong on employee communication and participation, including nonunion grievance methods, have better success in maintaining their status than those without such programs. While progressive human resources practices cannot be absolutely proven to have played a major part in declining union organization or certification, the inference seems clear.[7]

Problems occur when a company lacks a way to address employee complaints. Both formal and informal methods are needed so that employees will have a legitimate process that they perceive as fair—something better than the old complaint box. Surveys have shown that these kinds of internal problem-solving mechanisms are rare.[8]

What is needed are other designated employees who can serve as problem solvers on an informal basis. In some organizations, this will be the employee relations manager or other designated counselor; in others it will be a co-worker who has been designated to intervene. Where employee counselor systems have been instituted, management is positive about the ability of these liaison workers to solve problems and strengthen communication.[9]

There also needs to be a formal system with proscribed steps for resolving problems, such as mediation. When such systems are in place, communication is enhanced, morale is improved, and the need for outside representation is minimized.[10]

## SUMMARY

The key issue for human resources today is strategic alignment, redesigning jobs to reflect the service and quality aspects in today's organization. Job content, according to Hay Management consultant Bob Kosobud, is being changed to broaden content and recognize the new self-management aspects of a flattened organization. "Jobs now have more content and accountability," says Kosobud. "The new emphasis is on teamwork and leadership, and the question is 'who can survive and do well?' "[11]

The challenge of strategic human resources management is to help management develop the key messages—the *what*. The job of communication is to help figure out not how to get those messages to the work audience, but *how* to ensure they result in goal-oriented behaviors.

## ENDNOTES

1. Doron P. Levin, "Chrysler Factory Opens in Detroit," *New York Times*, April 1, 1992, p. A8.

2. Kathrine Lochridge and Melinda Bickerstaff, "The Restructuring Puzzle: Ways to Make the Pieces Fit," remarks delivered at the 1991 ASTD National Conference in San Francisco.

3. The ideas and linkages presented here are adapted from "In Concert," a seminar presented by Hay Communications, 1982.

4. Fred Thomson and Stuart McAdam, "Communicating When It Really Counts," *Director*, September 1988, pp. 139–40.

5. Frank Corrado and Sewell Gelberd, "Getting Back to Business," survivor recovery training program, 1991.

6. Jennier J. Laabs, "OLIVER: A Twist on Communication." *Personnel Journal*, September 1991, pp. 78–79.

7. Jack Fioriot, Christopher Lowman, and Forrest D. Nelson, "The Impact of Human Resources on Union Organizing," *Industrial Relations*, Spring 1987, pp. 113–26.

8. Alan F. Westin, "Justice Begins at Home," *Across the Board*, October 1984, pp. 50–54.

9. P.B. Marchall, "Employee Counselors—Opening New Lines of Communication, *Personnel Administrator*, November 1976, pp. 44–48.

10. Roger Madsen and Barbara Knudson-Fields, "Employee-Employer Relationships: When They Have a Cause to Complain," *Management Solutions*, April 1987, pp. 39–43.

11. Robert Kosobud, Hay Management Consultants. Interview with the author, Chicago, March 26, 1992.

## Chapter Six

# Communicating to the Marketplace

In the business of selling products to people, the aura in the firmament today is a term called *marketing public relations*. It refers to the maximum use of the news media to help sell products. The amazing growth of this part of the marketing promotion has come, to a great extent, from a widespread recognition in the U.S. marketing community that advertising by itself cannot solely bring products to market in an age known for a million messages a day and a resulting increase in consumer skepticism.

Marketing public relations has raised the cachet of the entire public-relations profession because of an ever-growing list of success stories:

- Campbell soup's public-relations program, "National Soup Month" resulted in a 36 percent increase in sales, the single biggest month's increase in Campbell's history.
- Selchow and Righter launched its Trivial Pursuit game by word of mouth and publicity and sold 22 million copies the first year.
- Diet Coke was launched with no advertising, but instead by a media blowout—Rockettes and all—at Radio City Music Hall.
- One woman's cosmetic company, The Body Shop, took a strong position on environmental issues and animal testing and saw sales grow like wildfire.

Marketing public relations has become a major success story not only for sellers of products and services, but also for the big public-relations agencies. According to one estimate, marketing communications now accounts for about 70 percent of the business handled by those agencies worldwide.[1]

In today's hostile environment, where consumers are hiding, as one public-relations person put it, "from the commercial rain of advertising messages,'' the demand for reaching key audiences makes public-relations people even more valuable.[2]

Public relations can have its impact in a number of ways. It can establish credibility and recognition up front for the advertising and promotion. It can strengthen the perception of the company and its products, while extending the reach and impact of the marketing. It can also provide a highly cost-effective adjunct to the effort.[3]

Marketing communications has long consisted of *advertising, sales promotion, and product publicity*. Product publicity has been around for most of the century. But today there is more fervor because of a strong belief that by using more sophisticated public relations, which works outside advertising channels, marketers can:

1. Pump new life into old products (Campbell's soup, Barbie).
2. Introduce new products (Gillette Sensor razor, Diet Coke, Cabbage Patch Dolls).
3. Reposition products (aspirin, Arm & Hammer).
4. Open up new markets (McDonald's in Moscow).
5. Provide third-party endorsements to advertising claims, via news stories (a consumer story on insects featuring Johnson's *Raid*).[4]

Public relations' new role is to help *create a receptive environment* for advertising and sales promotion. For example, selling cars in Japan is an advertising problem. Fostering a friendly environment in Japan for selling cars is a public-relations problem.

When the professors get together, they come up with the definition that public relations "builds and maintains hospitable social and political environments," while marketing "builds and maintains a market for an organization's goods and services."[5]

Some mark the start of the age of marketing public relations as 1982, when Johnson & Johnson deftly mounted a very credible public-relations effort to save its Tylenol brand after a series of deaths in Chicago (see Chapter 8 for the impact of the Tylenol incident on another major public-relations area— crisis communications). For the first time, the impact of excellent public relations on a consumer product was demonstrated clearly.[6]

Certainly, the Tylenol case gave a very visible boost to the importance of strategic communications in helping save a company's brand, but the move towards public relations in marketing has evolved over the past three decades.

## THE EVOLUTION OF MARKETING

Beginning in the 1960s, the concept of "lifestyle" marketing—marketing tied to the multiple interests of consumer groups—began to be identified. For example, drivers of high-priced cars, who are tennis or golf players and eat out at least two times a week, could be segmented.

Moreover, the concept of marketing was extended beyond products and services to organizations and high-profile people, like celebrities. During the 1970s, public-interest groups developed social-marketing campaigns based on environmental, food, safety and health, and rights issues. During this time, public relations really began to share the marketing environment.

Companies seeking to respond to public interest campaigns began utilizing issues, or advocacy advertising—to take a position on issues such as trade, media fairness, and attacks by an environmental group. Another major marketing concept of that era was Reis and Trout's positioning, which suggested that marketers had to fight for differentiation in people's minds. This led to the idea that linkage of a product to some type of public-relations effort, such as consumer service, would better position a product with users. Also in this period, growth occurred in the realm of marketing professional services, such as hospitals, legal and accounting firms, and strategic marketing of the organization, vis-à-vis societal issues such as education, regulatory reform, imports, and environment.

In the last decade, we witnessed the introduction of marketing warfare (again from Reis and Trout), which sought to position products by going head-to-head with competing brands—cola, beer, and tennis shoes, for example. Also, global marketing, and its opposite, city-by-city marketing, both gained adherents in this era. Direct marketing—door-to-door, shopping by TV and computer at home, and telemarketing—grew rapidly, as did the shop-at-home catalog business. Another major emphasis of the 1980s was relationship marketing: building personal relationships with customers through sporting and cultural events and sponsorships of public events. The hope was that because Philip Morris sponsored a major national celebration of the 200th anniversary of the Bill of Rights in 1991, for example, people would infer their shared values concerning personal freedoms in the United States, like the freedom to light up.[7]

## A BLENDING OF MARKETING AND PUBLIC RELATIONS

A combination of factors has resulted in the increasing use of public relations in marketing. One factor is *greater linkage by the public of issues like environment, health and safety, and respect for resources, to companies and products.* The big breakthroughs in marketing public relations, many say, came from the late 70s and early 80s when U.S. industry started having to respond to a wide number of public issues. At about the same time, lobbyists and political parties began utilizing high-end computer targeting and opinion sampling to identify issues and match them to constituencies, so that groups like the Moral Majority, for example, were able to generate hundreds of thousands of pieces of mail on an issue while it was pending in Congress.

Another factor is *the splintering of the mass market by the growth of cable television and the erosion of network television dominance.* About 70 percent of all homes in the United States now have VCRs, and around 50 percent have cable television with access to at least 50 channels.

A third factor is *a realization that advertising's credibility has eroded and that third-party endorsements in the media can restore some of that credibility.* An incredible amount of message clutter has been produced by advertising and the new communication/information technologies. As advertisers today are well aware, a man with a channel clicker and a short attention span is not a good sales prospect for an ad. (Many women will tell you that this trait is genetically specific to men.) Public opinion polls, for example, show that only 16 percent of consumers think TV and magazine advertisements are useful, and less than 27 percent think newspaper ads are of value.[8] Many years ago, the advertising guru David Ogilvy estimated that a news story about a product was six times more likely to be believed than an advertisement.[9] That observation seems to be even more valid today as people are bombarded continuously with commercial messages.

Occasionally, the news channels must be used to deal with negative information—from the government, from consumers, and from environmental and other interest groups. A company must fight back when it's named the top local discharger of toxic wastes or is put on the list of 10 worst polluters. A company is forced to prove an advertising claim of freshness, or disprove that its product claims don't hold up.

Where strategic corporate concerns have been ignored, a number of very memorable marketing disasters have occurred:

- Firestone, despite continued reports that its 500 radial tire was defective, stonewalled calls for a recall and Congressional inquiries. Only management bloodletting, recall of the tires, and the hiring of Jimmy Stewart as corporate spokesperson finally turned the situation around.
- The apple industry did not take seriously enough environmental group attacks on the use of the pesticide Alar, until "60 Minutes" raised the issue nationally and linked it with kids' health.
- The Suzuki Corporation continued to defend its Samurai vehicle after *Consumer Reports* raised concerns over the possibility it could tip on turns. After a big dip in sales, the company regained some market share, but quickly moved to redesign the vehicle.
- Source Perrier at first denied and then reacted slowly to reports of traces of benzene in its drinking water. After a belated recall, the product returned, but never regained its previous market share.

Marketing has become dependent, not only on public relations, but on *strategic corporate communication* to help get past serious public issues that can directly impact sales: the StarKist policy on dolphin-safe tuna, a beer company's advertising on safe driving, and McDonald's decision to end plastic packaging are recent examples.

## MARKETING PUBLIC RELATIONS' FUNCTION

Some questions must be asked before developing an integrated marketing campaign:

- What specific consumer behavior do you seek to change?
- What audiences do you need to reach?
- What's the primary message you want to deliver?
- What key messages do you want to deliver to targeted audiences?
- What's the best way to marshal public relations, promotion, and advertising to deliver the messages?
- How can these activities achieve creativity and synergy?[10]

Marketing public relations delivers sales messages by another door— news and public affairs—areas that still have the ability to grab and hold people's attention and present a credible message.

Reaching target audiences goes well beyond just getting stories in the paper. It extends to special events, consumer information, and sponsorship.

Marketing public relations assists the marketing effort with a number of different kinds of tactics:

1. Media tours.
2. TV, magazine, radio, newspaper publicity.
3. News events.
4. Seminars and workshops.
5. Event sponsorships (arts, sports, celebrations).
6. Brochures.
7. Public service campaigns.
8. Videos, videoconferences, and video news releases.

Today, the product message is aggressively sold for news and features stories. For example, Johnson's *"Raid"* became the example for a story on summer insects and how to fight them; a cigarette company sponsored a jazz festival (Kool) or a tennis tournament (Virginia Slims); an insurance company sponsored a golf tournament (Kemper); and everybody sponsors a college bowl (take your pick). All generate news coverage and the ad is in the title.

Public relations is perfect for today's environment of cluttered messages, global business expansion, and public-interest concerns on a wide range of issues—from fur coats to safe driving to waste reduction. It provides the tools for dealing with those issues in the public arena and can help position the product for maximum visibility and public support.

Thanks to new technologies, news reporters can pick up corporate video news releases (VNRs) via satellite, receive news releases via data terminal and fax, and even participate in national satellite news conferences right from their offices. In an environment where media owners have become especially cautious about spending money, this approach has worked to the advantage of the marketing communicator.

A simple example of this process comes in the form of a video news release for agricultural communities, in which an herbicide manufacturer sends out, via satellite, a news piece on a new product that is helping with resistant strains of common weeds. Included in the package is footage of farmers tilling, an interview with an agricultural university researcher, for credibility, and a second sound bite of the sales director for the manufacturer. The package is produced in such a way that the local station can use its own reporter to do the voice in the background. Via fax or computer, written copy is sent, making it almost effortless for the TV station to run the story. The public-relations agency conducts follow-up to see how many stations ran the piece.

For a cost of about $10,000, companies can produce and broadcast, via satellite services like Medialink, a video news release to 548 subscribing stations across the United States. In addition, another 200 are contacted. This means the release reached three fourths of U.S. TV markets. Comparable advertising time on network stations runs as high as $100,000 per spot.[11]

To budget-conscious marketers, the best news is that marketing public relations costs are only a fraction of advertising expenses and can pay off handsomely. One of the most famous stories is how Selchow and Righter, with little money available to launch the parlor game, Trivial Pursuit, sent to celebrities copies of the game cards on which their names appeared. This helped build word-of-mouth publicity as did giveaways of the games via radio disc jockeys whose listeners could answer questions from the game. A media tour of 125 stations was arranged for the game's creators, and Trivial Pursuit fundraising parties for Easter Seals were sponsored in 80 U.S. cities before the first selling season. First-year sales were 22 million, with hardly an ad.[12]

Prognosticators see more of the same for the future, with ever-greater growth for public-relations marketing. They cite continued increases in regulation as well as global communication and continued public initiatives to make companies responsible. The danger is that too much emphasis on marketing public relations will eventually kill the goose that laid the golden egg. Already, there are moves afoot to limit advertorials and infomercials on television.

The fact that television news has been made into a profit center by the changing economics and increased competitiveness of the TV business has probably contributed as much to the growth of marketing as anything else. Overuse could substantially hurt the credibility of the news business. A study by Northwestern University students in a single day of programming found 818 instances of a recognizable product, or mention of a brand or corporate name. News programs accounted for 44 percent, variety shows had 24 percent, and news features accounted for 14 percent. The study said that the most mentions came during the early morning news programs like "Today" and "Good Morning America."[13]

## DEVELOPING A MARKETING COMMUNICATIONS GAME PLAN

Fitting public relations into a marketing program is not difficult. Here are some broad guidelines:

1. Public relations should be part of the overall organizational approach to selling goods and services. This means that it has to be an integrated part of the entire marketing process.
2. The approach needs to fit with the overall marketing strategy. Simply put, the public-relations aspects must have a clearly defined role in the campaign.
3. Some sort of evaluation component should be built in to test the impact of marketing communications. The easy answer here is that if sales increase you know you've succeeded. But like America's first department store mogul, John Wannamaker, used to say, "I know I'm wasting half of my advertising dollars, but I don't know which half." Measurement can help find out how effective both marketing and public relations were.
4. Public relations people should be involved at a very strategic level—to be able not only to generate publicity, but also to position the product, protect it from attack, or give it new life.

## MEASUREMENT AND EVALUATION

The traditional ways of measuring product publicity were quite crude:

- Count the number of total column inches a story garnered.
- Count the number of publications carrying a story.
- Add up broadcast time and number of stations.
- Sum up exposure by adding readership to viewership to listenership for a total number of consumer impressions.
- Show what comparable purchased time, or advertising, costs would have been.

While these stats can be impressive, they don't necessarily indicate impact on sales. The problem becomes a Catch-22 situation, however, because marketing public relations costs so much less than advertising—

**FIGURE 6–1**
*Behavior Change Model*

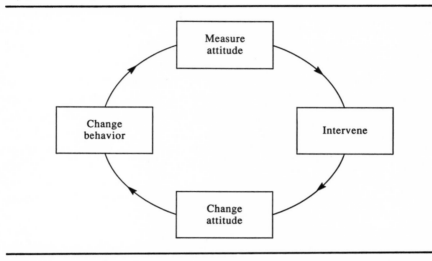

as little as 10 percent of the advertising budget (which is already a fraction of the total marketing budget). Therefore, from a financial perspective, it is not cost-effective to spend the kind of money on evaluation of marketing communications that you might with advertising. Burson-Marstellar's Lloyd Kirban estimates that costs for test-market measurements can be about 10 percent of the total campaign cost.

The measurement tools are basically the same for advertising and marketing public relations—to discern changes in consumer behavior via control and test markets, and to utilize before-and-after surveys and focus groups to measure impact.

According to Kirban, the important issue is whether you can measure communication variance—the specific impact a message has on people. Clipping counts and estimated numbers of impression only measure awareness. They don't look at movement towards goal-oriented action.[14]

The need is to design models that not only measure attitudes, but show behavior change. (See Figure 6–1.)

Northwestern University's Philip Kolter suggests that the similarities are so strong between advertising and public relations that common behavioral measures such as focus groups, concept testing, and copy and media tests can be used for both.[15]

Many public relations professionals seem to evaluate effectiveness by Kentucky windage—"by guess and by golly." Some believe it is good enough to be able to point to "greater sales than expected" as a measure of success. In the description of a successful launch of a new air freshener, the results reported a generation of 115 million impressions at a cost per impression of $0.014. The campaign had exceeded the company's expectation, gaining a 20 percent market share, which was considered exceptional considering a high-priced item for a saturated market. Naturally, a lot of questions remain concerning whether that 20 percent increase remained over time.[16]

One public-relations professional, who very much supports measurement, described the roll-out of a prescription allergy product in which public relations was pegged to the top 20 allergy markets in the United States utilizing a mall tour. Before the campaign, consumer focus groups were conducted as well as individual interviews with doctors and allergists to ensure the materials would work with all groups. After some modifications and FDA approval, the focus groups and interviews were conducted in the first two markets of the tour. The objective was to find the level of target audience action—to find the relationship between exposure to the campaign and sales.

According to Patricia Newlin, a public-relations counselor, of those exposed to the publicity, 83 percent recalled the announcement; about half recalled key product benefits such as no drowsiness and no side effects; three quarters said they would ask their doctors about the product; 5 per cent were prescribed the product by doctors during the three-month period of the study; and sales exceeded objectives. Newlin suggests that the public relations industry stop talking about evaluation and just do it.[17]

Criticism of public relations evaluation comes from long-time public-relations educator Philip Lesly, who points to a trend by management towards measurability and computer-driven facts to "the visible and tangible" rather than "the nuances of human feelings and emotions." As a result of this "schizophrenia," he predicts that public relations will probably go on growing in numbers, but slipping in stature and influence.

He argues that the most valuable thing public relations can do is not measurable—helping organizations avoid mistakes, advising reconciliation over conflict, shaping positions and perceptions. To people who live by the numbers, this value is ignored.[18]

## WHO DOES WHAT

How should corporate communications and marketing relate to each other in the organization?

Which model of organization makes the most sense—in other words, who's in charge here? The answer may come from viewing communications as a *staff* function, and marketing as a *line* function.

Some say the public-relations component of corporate communications should be part of marketing; others say the reverse; some suggest both activities have their own lives to lead, but ought to get together when necessary. In an earlier time, each function had distinct responsibilities that were not perceived to have an intersection beyond the need for product publicity to support sales.

In today's more complex information and communication society, however, where an educated public has strong interests in issues such as product safety, race relation, the environment, product value, and customer service, an environment exists that can easily be hostile to marketing of products and services that step on those concerns, such as cigarettes and beer, for example.

At the same time, the odds are not insurmountable. Companies can turn a problem to their own advantage, by capitalizing on the issue and delivering a credible differing opinion. The Beef Industry Council has had to overcome strong negative perceptions that its product is a cause of heart disease. The Chemical Manufacturers Association has become preemptive in managing environmental community relations with its Responsible Care™ program. Honda Motors conducted an aggressive campaign to emphasize its "Made in America" automobiles in the wake of calls for bans on Japanese imports.

*Corporate public relations* is concerned with the societal environment in which the business operates. *Marketing public relations* is involved in the environment only as it can be made friendly for selling. In this age of more socially conscious consumers, there will be instances when marketing will need to take second place to overall corporate interests. A company that gets in trouble over an environmental issue, such as the dolphin/tuna issue, will need to make strategic decisions about corporate practices and then credibly communicate them to the public. Marketing public relations needs to deal with the problem.

The future will not get any easier. Organizations, such as the New York-based Council on Economic Priorities, are publishing guides to companies, products and services that rate them on a wide number of issues: charitable giving, right to know, end to apartheid, environmental commitment, conservation and better energy packaging, community concerns, and commitment to equal employment. The paperback book containing the ratings, entitled *Shopping for a Better World*, has sold nearly a million copies since it was first published.[19]

Corporate communications, as a senior staff function, is best positioned to provide a *strategic* perspective that should not be expected of a line function such as marketing. The marketing perspective should be very focused on product sales strategies. A company that does not maintain a strong *strategic* communications staff function will suffer in a difficult situation. As one expert noted, "Marketing says we either meet the needs and drives of the customer, agree to a 'win-win' and make the exchange, or we are nowhere. Public relations says we either build relationships and make some accommodations, or we are nowhere."[20]

The job of corporate communication is to deal with government, the interest groups, opinion makers and key influential people and groups, and the media. It's marketing's job to work with the advertisers and the media to target the consumers. Certainly, an argument can be made that the marketing part of public relations makes sense being housed in marketing, especially in light of the dramatic changes going on with the fragmentation of mass markets and the perceived decline of advertising effectiveness. At the same time, the corporation is playing on a bigger stage these days and has public relations needs beyond marketing. The answer might be that public relations should be split, with the staff function having higher rank.[21]

Since a great amount of an organization's marketing communication work is usually done by outside counsel, the highest level of activity for the marketing public-relations person inside the organization is establishing the strategic *message platform*, the basis from which all marketing public relations emanates. That platform describes the behaviors that are to be changed.

### How to Get Started

Michael O. Niederquell of Anthony M. Franco, Inc. suggests a six-step process to introduce marketing public relations.

1. Set up a system. Appoint a gatekeeper who can bring all the components of the marketing mix together. That person should be a strategic

communicator, such as the marketing director or the public relations director.

2. Strategically evaluate. Look at the marketing environment from a public relations perspective. This will give you a chance to identify issues and obstacles that will have to be looked at and planned for.

3. Factor specific public-relations components into the plan. This will help deal with potential conflicts the company may face from a company, product, management, or service perspective.

4. Target. Utilize public-relations' capability to reach specific target groups through the clutter with a credible message.

5. Be open to ideas. It might be necessary for advertising to be muted or not even used, depending on the situation and the issues involved, especially with environmental concerns.[22]

## SUMMARY

Communication, in the form of marketing public relations, creates value today by providing a more credible approach than advertising in the selling of products. By using news media channels, companies also can extend the reach of their marketing. Marketing public relations may have its greatest impact, though, on creating an environment for successful sales. In a time in which social, environmental, trade, and safety issues can have a negative effect on sales, marketing public relations can help companies build relationships and influence perceptions. In a time when markets are more fragmented and customers more sophisticated, public relations is creating value.

## ENDNOTES

1. Scott M. Cutlip, "The Invasion of Public Relations' Domain by Lawyers and Marketers," *IABC Communications World*, January 1992, pp. 25–28. The 70 percent is broken down into consumer products (20%), industrial (15%), entertainment (10%), business-to-business (5%), and health care (5%).

2. Michael O. Neiderquell, "Integrating the Strategic Benefits of Public Relations into the Marketing Mix," *Public Relations Quarterly*, Spring 1991, pp. 23–4.

3. *Ibid.*

4. Prema Nakra, "The Changing Role of Public Relations in Marketing Communications," *Public Relations Quarterly*, Spring 1991, pp. 42–45.

5. Glen M. Broom, Martha M. Lauzen, and Kerry Tucker, "Public Relations and Marketing: Dividing the Conceptual Domain and Operational Turf," *Public Relations Review*, Fall 1991, pp. 219–25.

6. Nakra, "The Changing Role of Public Relations in Marketing Communications," p. 42A.

7. Adapted from Kotler in Thomas Harris', *The Marketer's Guide to Public Relations* (New York: John Wiley & Sons, 1991), pp. 279–83.

8. *Ibid*, p. 23.

9. David Ogilvy, *Ogilvy on Advertising* (New York: Crown Publishers, 1983), p. 90.

10. Mary R. Trudel, "Consumer Marketing Synergy: PR Comes of Age," *Public Relations Quarterly*, Spring 1991, pp. 18–19.

11. "Prefab News," *Technology Review*, October, 1989, p. 6.

12. Harris, *The Marketer's Guide to Public Relations*, p. 137.

13. "Free Plugs Supply Ad Power," *Advertising Age*, January 29, 1990, p. 6.

14. Frank M. Corrado, *Media for Managers* (Englewood Cliffs, New Jersey: Prentice-Hall, 1984), pp. 24–25.

15. Philip Kotler, *Marketing for Nonprofit Organizations* (Englewood-Cliffs, New Jersey: 1982), pp. 572–91.

16. James B. Strenski, "Marketing Public Relations Sells: Case Studies Prove It," *Public Relations Quarterly*, Spring 1991, pp. 25–26.

17. Patricia E. Newlin, "A Public Relations Measurement and Evaluation Model That Finds the Movement of the Needle," *Public Relations Quarterly*, Spring 1991, pp. 40–41.

18. Philip Lesly, "Public Relations in the Turbulent New Human Climate," *Public Relations Review*," Spring 1991, pp. 1–8.

19. The Council on Economic Priorities, *Shopping for a Better World* (New York: Ballantine Books, 1992).

20. Patrick Jackson quoted in Broom, et al., "Public Relations and Marketing: Dividing the Conceptual Domain and Operational Turf," 1991.

21. Robert L. Dilenschneider, "Marketing Communications in the Post-Advertising Era," *Public Relations Review*, Fall 1991, pp. 227–36.

22. Michael O. Niederquell, "Integrating the Strategic Benefits of Public Relations in the Marketing Mix," pp. 23–24.

## Chapter Seven

# The Green Manager

"I think we must . . . keep our environment liveable. The challenge is: How do we stay in business while this is accomplished?" asked the president of a small metal-products firm.

"The EPA has made our life hell for no good reason. . . . I have grown totally fed up and cynical about 'environmentalism,' " said the president of a small electrical-equipment manufacturing company.[1]

But, as Monsanto Co.'s Chairman Richard J. Mahoney told *Business Week*, "Sometimes you find that the public has spoken, and you get on with it."[2]

While marketers see it as a boom, operations managers see it as their bane. Either way, the environmental movement is continuing to have a significant impact on U.S. industry.

Renewed public support for improvement is driving the momentum. A 1991 poll found that more than half of Americans were willing to sacrifice jobs to fight pollution, and a similar percentage said they would ante up more money for environmental safe products and practices, including safe garbage disposal. The poll also reported that 64 percent favored "mandatory jail sentences for decision makers in any organization that fails to comply with environmental regulations after receiving a warning.

The success of U.S. business in creating value has, to a great extent, come from the abundance of this nation's natural resources. But as the basic needs and wants of the American people have been met and the land has been tamed, new concerns have arisen for a more caring husbandry of resources.

Negative effects of America's rapid population growth and industrialization have been felt worldwide. An earthmosphere plagued by greenhouse warming, a widening hole in the ozone layer, and vanishing forests that regenerate oxygen are symptoms of imbalance in nature.

The great pollution icons of the last two decades are familiar to most Americans—Lake Erie on fire, boarded up homes at Love Canal, oil on the birds on Alaska's Kenai peninsula, hypodermic needles on the Jersey shore, poison gas at Bhopal, and fiery oil wells in Kuwait.

At the community level, adoption by a great number of people in the industrialized world of an environmental ethic in the wake of these and other incidents and accidents is having deep impacts on business decision making. Before it runs its course, the green movement may dramatically alter the basic business ethic of continuing growth and development.

The world environmental summit in Rio in 1992 emphasized the need for "sustainable development." This concept stresses that future economic prosperity depends on wisely using natural resources and balancing human activity with the ability of nature to renew itself. There are implications for all nations—industrial nations need to use their technology to develop ways to consume less; developing nations need to cut birth rates and use their land and resources more wisely.[3]

Today, 76 percent of Americans identify themselves as environmentalists. Activists call the 1990s the environmental decade. In his first presidential campaign, George Bush claimed he would be the environmental president. Public opinion polling on environmental issues shows, in ironic fashion, the environmental slogan, "think globally, act loyally." The public strongly supports environmental cleanup, but when it impacts their backyard, they often backpeddle.[4] The 20th anniversary celebration of Earth Day in 1990 has also generated momentum.

Citizen action in major cities around the United States sparked the first Earth Day and the legislation that generated environmental cleanup in the United States in 1970. Between 1970 and 1980, an estimated $1 trillion was spent on pollution controls. Today, environmental cleanup represents a $25 billion segment of the economy.[5]

Business has not been in a hurry to get out front on the environmental issue. This is somewhat understandable in light of a general perception in the business community that environmental compliance is difficult enough, so if you stumble and fall, it's better to do so in the shadows than in the sunlight.

However, business is becoming more visible on environmental issues, like it or not. One reason is that federal legislation, like EPA's SARA Title III, requires companies to report annually how much in toxics they put into the local atmosphere.

At the same time, companies have realized that there is money to be made in the marketplace for a company that can link their products or services to environmental improvement.

A major study by Booz Allen & Hamilton showed that most companies don't even have a written environmental policy.[6] Only 7 percent of executives surveyed said they felt very comfortable that the environmental issues facing their company were well understood, or that an adequate risk management was in place to handle them. The study concluded that most companies have a reactive approach that focuses on cleaning up abandoned sites, minimizing liabilities, and achieving compliance. Threat, not opportunity, drives environmental policy, the study concluded.

Only a few of the 200 Fortune 500 companies that responded said they were making an attempt to tell their story to the public, though the study concluded that "effective public relations is inseparable from a successful environmental program." The study further concluded that companies need to develop and execute a strategy to promote opportunities and moderate risk concerns.

A company that appears to have a green flag flying and is proactive on environmental issues may have an easier time getting approval for siting a facility. Being perceived as environmentally friendly can also pay off with consumers as well as employees. As far as employees go, the study suggested that environmental concerns need to be integrated into the core values and culture of the organization.

Washington environmental public affairs specialist E. Bruce Harrison believes that in today's environment, where green issues have high visibility, companies that do the right thing technically regarding green issues can still lose the public relations game, as Exxon CEO Lawrence Rawls discovered with the Valdez disaster. Says Harrison, "The human factor is particularly powerful in environmental affairs, often outweighing science, logic, or even facts."[7]

Harrison notes how green issues have affected a wide number of business sectors:

- Banking—Officials must decide whether a commercial customer will inherit or develop environmental problems that could create heavy liabilities.

- Health care—Managers face problems in disposing of medical and radiological wastes.

- Science—The scientific process has been exposed as equivocal, as environment, nutrition, and global warming issues show how ambiguous scientific evidence can be. Tests that include injecting mice with large dosages of chemicals are questioned by the public.

The media have read the polls that say three out of four Americans consider themselves environmentalists and have gone on the attack. Therefore, business must be more *proactive* in reconciling its need to service customers with its environmental stance, both internally and externally. This proactive stance includes establishing an environmental policy, bringing the company into compliance, telling its story to the community and other groups, and taking advantage of market opportunities.


## POSITIVE GREEN ATTITUDE

"If we made a lot of money destroying the planet, we sure can make money cleaning it up," said an environmental official for Loblaw Co. of Toronto at an Advertising Age meeting in New York.[8]

Besides promoting green marketing, companies are waving the flags of pollution prevention. Pollution prevention encourages companies to reduce their emissions and releases into the environment.

A more positive attitude can even be seen in pollution laws. The new Clean Air Act, for example, includes not only strategies designed to encourage companies to reduce their waste streams, but also to accumulate and trade pollution credits or allowances. The Chicago Board of Trade was planning to create a market to buy and sell SO2 emissions. This program might allow trading of smokestack emissions for clean cars and give credit for mobile source improvements that are made faster than what is required by law.

Generally, new pollution laws are emphasizing establishment of market-based and results-oriented approaches, rather than detailing methodologies and techniques.

If an organization is looking to create a proactive environmental program, it needs to follow these four rules:

1. Develop a written environmental policy and really implement it within the organization.

2. Get out in front of the issues. Demonstrate publicly to constituencies that the company is doing things.

3. Communicate actions. Aggressively tell the company's story.

Members of the company environmental team should include top management, operations, research and development (R&D) and engineering, regulatory, legal, and communications, as well as marketing and human resources when needed.

Companies that have taken the lead in these programs have been the consumer products companies such as McDonald's Corporation and Proctor & Gamble (P & G). In 1991, McDonald's was criticized for using plastic packaging. After some brief hesitation, the company switched from polystyrene to paper products. Shortly thereafter, it was reported that the polystyrene was probably less environmentally damaging. But, because of its high visibility and the perception that McDonald's was trying to do the right thing, little criticism followed.

National polls have indicated that P & G is the number one environmentally conscious company in the United States. P & G's environmental approach is aimed at waste management, especially source reduction, waste-to-energy, composting, and recycling. Part of this effort is a defensive reaction to the continued criticism of its Pampers disposable diaper line.

Other proactive environmental efforts by numerous businesses have included: (1) good neighbor programs such as conservation and process changes that reduce use of resources and cut pollution, (2) office recycling programs for paper and glass that involves all employees, and (3) the use of recycled paper and soy-based inks in publications.

Here are five tips for improving corporate environmental communications:

1. *Become an environmental expert.* Learn the technical language and major environmental issues and terms such as the difference between the Resource Conservation and Recover Act (RCRA), which deals with newly generated wastes, and CERCLA (Comprehensive Environmental Resource Conservation and Liability Act) or simply, the Superfund Law, which deals with hazardous waste sites.

2. *Establish lines to local and national groups.* Get to know the local and national environmental organizations and their key leaders. Major players include, among others, the Natural Resources Defense Council, the Sierra Club, and the Environmental Defense Fund. Also get together

with local groups to find out who their leaders are and establish personal contact.

3. *Use credible publicity.* Deal straightforwardly with reporters on environmental issues. Brief reporters on future programs, and tell them the good news with the bad. Also spend time with reporters when technical issues are involved to make sure they get the story right.

4. *Get employees on your side.* Employees are concerned about environmental issues at their company. When properly informed, they can also help tell the company's story in their community.

5. *Know your community.* Learn what are the main environmental concerns in your community and find out where your organization fits.[9]

## MARKETING IN GREEN

Companies are making money through green marketing. They have switched to recycled packaging, established in-house recycling programs, and developed environmentally sound products. Smart organizations have begun to use environmental principles to sell products.

This move to go "green" is the result of a realization that the public is committed to environmentally safe products. Companies such as Tom's of Maine, The Body Shop, and others have built successful niches with environmentally safe products. Researchers predict *green* will be to the 1990s market what *lite* was to the 1980s market. Currently, it is estimated that the green market represents about 5 to 10 percent of the $500 billion a year market in food and beverage sales in the United States. Eventually, that number might grow to as much as 30 percent.[10] And today, many also believe that the more customers know about a company's environmental initiatives, the more positive their response will be.

The rush by many companies in the last few years to claim that they are green brought requests that the Federal Trade Commission set standards and define words such as *recyclable, degradable, compostable,* and the like. Sweeping statements such as "environmentally safe" or "earth friendly," also raised concern because of a general belief that no man-made product can be completely harmless. More specific phrases like "recyclable where collection programs exist" were recommended.[11]

A 1992 study found that a majority of European consumers, though willing to pay more for less environmentally damaging products, and willing to sacrifice some quality to buy a product that would cause less damage, were generally skeptical of "green" claims by manufacturers whom they perceived as "simply jumping on the environmental bandwagon."[12]

Polls in the United States show that Americans very much want objective information on the environmental impact of products they buy. Two nonprofit organizations have moved to develop seals similar to the Underwriters Laboratory (UL) mark. As a matter of fact, UL was behind the development of the Green Seal mark, designed to be awarded to certain categories of products that meet environmental standards. Early categories up for consideration were toilet and facial tissues and motor oil. By late 1991, a similar label, Green Cross, had already certified 400 products produced by 80 companies.[13]

## PLANNING TO GO GREEN

A study by the Conference Board has shown that more than 70 percent of 350 companies in a national poll had formal systems in place to identify key environmental issues.[14]

Companies that want to "go green" are advised to use a process similar to the following:

1. *Make a commitment.* Get your top managers together to take a look at how your company fits in the world about it, and how it is perceived by customers, employees, government regulators, and the public.

2. *Develop a plan.* Decide what your company is doing at present in the way of environmental initiatives. Evaluate all your programs—from in-house recycling to manufacturing, packaging, distribution, and waste disposal.

3. *Audit your operation.* You might bring in a professional for this. Take a look at whether you're in compliance with all state and federal regulations, what some potential pitfalls may be, what the opportunities are for waste reduction and packaging improvements, all the way through to material substitution in manufacturing and recycling.

4. *Name a Green Chief.* Name an environmental czar who has technical capability, and also authority and commitment to implement change and motivate people. These traits are hard to find in one person. Some would advise using an engineer or scientist for this position. You

may need a salesperson for the job. Keep the technical person involved in environmental compliance issues, not in moving the company towards a green ethic.

5. *Involve employees*. You're going to have lots of support and goodwill from employees, especially from the younger ones. They will go out of their way to support the program and brag about it.

6. *Spread the word*. Don't just promote the program internally, tell the world. 3M corporation has focused on process changes (such as substituting water base for solvent base in products) to reduce pollution emissions by a billion pounds while saving $500 million in costs. They have been very aggressive in telling that story around the world.[15]


## BEING CREDIBLE

A company attempting to position itself in the marketplace as environmentally committed can expect to be more closely scrutinized by the media when it occasionally slips. Adolph Coors Co., which had led a national campaign to clean up water pollution, was investigated in the late 1980s for allegedly hiding the fact that leaky pipes at one of its plants had contaminated nearby springs. Also, safety accidents like a plant explosion can tarnish the image of an environmentally committed company.

Federal requirements mandating disclosure of a company's toxic emission have given unwanted visibility to many companies. Those companies argue that toxicity is more of a problem than just volume. A company that puts out tens of thousands of solvents each year, for example, may really be less of a polluter than a company that puts out 3,000 pounds of toxics each year such as lead or cadmium. Yet the federal reporting rules of the Emergency Planning and Community Right-to-Know Act of 1986 (SARA Title III) emphasizes quantity of pollutant over quality. This makes it easy for the media—and the community—to misplace concern.[16]

Companies with high emission numbers can also run into trouble with the financial markets. Most investors are motivated less by environmental considerations than by the belief that significant emitters are inefficient producers. ''The feeling is that companies that emit a lot of toxic waste do not have good financial indicators long term,'' one analyst remarked.[17]

# COMMUNICATING WITH COMMUNITIES

We live in an age of NIMBY ("not in my backyard") when it comes to the siting of all kinds of public and private projects: from fast-food outlets to incinerators, to airport expansion, to power lines and waste disposal sites.

The public, conditioned by television, has very negative, preformed opinions. Those in government charged with managing the process are underfunded and undertrained, and do not have a workable process for involving the public in the decision-making process. Elected officials use the issues in an opportunistic manner. And the public has a craving for a riskless world.

Impacted publics know how to fight smart when defending their community against public and private developers. These individuals are often highly educated. They understand zoning and other administrative procedures and are savvy about manipulating the media to maximize their impact on the political process. Part of the problem is that these citizens have come to greatly mistrust the political process and feel compelled to step in to protect their own interests.[18]

As a result, only 1 of 10 proposed landfills gets built in the United States.[19] Attempts to build incinerators, which are considered safer to both humans and the environment than landfills, are invariably subject to even greater community outrage. In noting how difficult it is for a major city to site jails, drug treatment centers, and other unpopular land uses, former New York Mayor Ed Koch called the refusal by local community leaders to share the burdens that government imposes on all its citizens the start of a "new age of feudalism" that will fragment the country.[20]

Because of the NIMBY syndrome, community residents worried about property values and health effects find an easy enemy to unite against. Government and industry generally attempt to counter local opposition with ineffective public meetings and hearings, where scores of technical specialists are available to answer questions, but do not really involve the public in the process. Community groups, often with help from a number of national organizations that provide outside expertise, move quickly to attack the siting process in the press, in the hearings, and in the courts.

Organizations that attempt to site facilities have found that the most difficult locations tend to be those with an affluent, upscale, well-educated population. Though not always true, organizations have encountered less resistance in areas with a stronger blue-collar, low-to-middle-income population.

There are a lot of reasons why siting NIMBYs have not been more successful, but certainly some of the problem can be blamed on the government's window-dressing approach to public involvement. In many instances, the public is presented with a take it or leave it decision, with no chance to impact that decision.

Local citizens want a say in decisions that may impact their health or property values. Citizens will not become extremists if they are involved in the decision-making process that will impact them. They've seen how communities are impacted by hazardous waste dumps like Love Canal, New York, and Times Beach, Missouri, and they are wary of government and industry cleanup programs.

The burden is on government and industry to seek out these people, attempt to get them meaningfully involved, and actually listen to their ideas. People who believe they are getting the "bum's rush" from a governmental agency will reject participation in the process.

For anybody involved in a siting activity, the cardinal rule is "the process is the message." Success is not guaranteed, but it is possible, if those who are potentially affected feel that they are being dealt with fairly and credibly. The theory, proven many times over, is that if those being impacted feel that they are being given a fair hearing and are being listened to, they will be less resistant to fight, and may choose not to contest a final decision that is adverse to their interest.

The downside of this process is that it takes a lot of time, people, and money. It is rare today for even 5 percent of the budget of a major project to be spent on any kind of public-involvement activities. Ten percent is recommended.

The typical mistake made by government is to believe that a public meeting or hearing will take care of its public-involvement obligations. An even bigger mistake industry often makes is to rely on government to take the lead in public involvement activities.

Public meetings are among the *least* effective of all community relations techniques. Meetings tend to create an atmosphere of "us versus them." By the time a public meeting is held, most positions have been solidified. Citizens usually have little opportunity to have their questions answered, and the answers given are often vague (Can you guarantee my kids won't get cancer from the emissions? Will pollution leach through the ground to the water supply?).

Box 7–1

*Public Involvement in the 1990s*

*What's In*
• Targeted marketing of issues to various community interest groups.
• Negotiation.
• Informal small group communication.

*What's Out*
• Tack-on citizen programs at the end of a program or project.
• Single definitions of "public."
• Formal meetings and hearings.
• Neglect of risk issues.

When answers are not forthcoming or are hedged, the group, led by activists, can become openly hostile. The meeting often becomes adversarial and confrontational. The media in attendance begin covering the event like it was a sporting match, evaluating who scored the most points. Often, the event leads to no resolution. By letting the government take the lead, industry ends up at the mercy of other players.

Attempts have been made by some agencies to better *lead* this process. These agencies have introduced negotiation and conflict-resolution approaches with some success. They have successfully used one-on-one activities such as tours, small group meetings, hotlines, and on-scene representatives.

In the end, people who are being called on to accept a risky project are probably going to have to be compensated for accepting that risk. (See the section on risk.)

## MANAGING ENVIRONMENTAL MEETINGS

For the organization facing a public meeting, there are a number of proactive steps to take that will minimize the damage. The most important thing it can do is hold smaller meetings *beforehand* to establish relationships with people and acquaint them with the issues. Large group meetings are not an effective forum for communication. Their primary purpose is usually to bring community attention to an issue. Groups will use them to put on a show for the media, and they rarely produce satisfying results for any affected party. Sometimes, however, as in the case of a public hearing, there is no option.

In the fall of 1991, the U.S. and Ohio EPAs scheduled back-to-back public meetings and hearings in East Liverpool, Ohio, on the request of a company to build a waste incinerator. Because of poor advance preparation, the agencies allowed citizen opponents to completely upend the process. During the public meeting the first night, citizens refused to participate, and kept the media entertained outside while 15 or more agency representatives waited in a cavernous, but mostly empty, auditorium to answer questions. The second night, a public stenographer and hearing official were shouted off the stage by the same raucous group. "The public participation process is a sham," yelled one citizen leader into the closest microphone. Avoiding this kind of situation requires intense involvement and lots of time on the part of all parties, long before any meetings are held.

If you are meeting with the public in a potentially contentious situation, here are some suggestions for getting you through the process:

1. Before the meeting starts, get out on the floor and introduce yourself to people. Establish one-on-one rapport.

2. Organize your presentation and limit the key points you want to make to three or four.

3. Talk in a conversational way, without jargon. Also talk in terms of your audience's interests. They need to know what's in it for them.

4. Don't "take the bait" of answering hostile or leading questions. Call it for what it is and bridge over to amplify one of your key points.

The real secret to successful public involvement activities is to recognize that this is an exercise in *participatory democracy* and thus to establish a process that recognizes this truth. An effective process involves early identification of key participants, seeking a win-win solution based on mutual interests, overcommunicating information to audiences to prevent surprises, and involving the public in the entire decision process from start to finish.

**FIGURE 7-1**
*Historic Trends in Decision Making*

| Trends in Decision-Making | | |
|---|---|---|
| Organization decides<br><br>    Organization consults with individuals or experts | | |
| | Organization consults with representative group and decides | |
| | | Organization works with representative group and jointly decides<br><br>    Public Vote Regulation Legislation Litigation |
| Public involvement process | | |
| Decide, announce defend | Review and comment | Open decision process |

───────── Historic Trend ─────────▶

Source: *U.S. Bureau of Reclamation, Mid-Pacific Region, Public Involvement Training Resource Notebook, 1992.*

Figure 7-1 points out that the trend today in decision making on public issues has evolved from an authoritarian, "decide, announce, defend" approach to a more open process that is more interactive.

Figure 7-2 shows that public involvement activity and interest grow, the farther along into the decision process you go. The challenge is to have a representative process that soon captures enough involvement and maintains credibility later when there is more interest.

## RISK COMMUNICATION

The major issues in risk communication are *perception* and *credibility*. If you go to a public meeting and a government official tells you the water is safe to drink, you may or may not believe him. But if a local medical

**FIGURE 7-2**
*Public Involvement as a Process*

Decision Process                          Public Involvement
                                          Activity

Internal Decision Strategy

Describe Problems and Needs

Identify Issues and Publics

Finalize Decision Strategy

Formulate Alternatives

Evaluate Alternatives

Identify Implementable Solutions

Make Recommendation

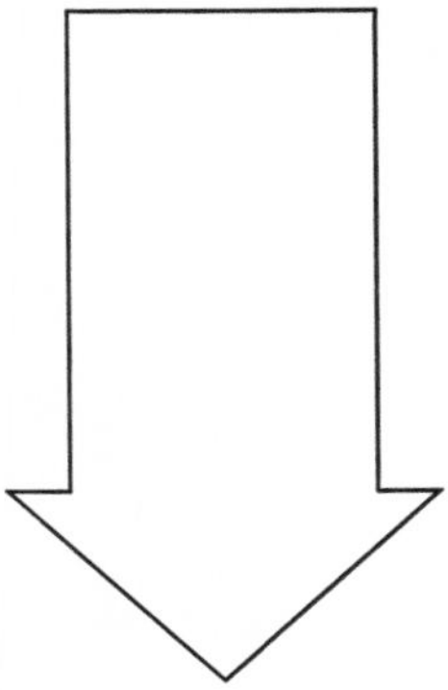

Source: *U.S. Bureau of Reclamation, Mid-Pacific Region, Public Involvement Training Resource Notebook, 1992.*

doctor stands up and says not to worry about the drinking water, you are more likely to believe him. Credibility is probably the reason. On the other hand, if you've visited the scene or looked at some of the murky stuff in a bottle before the meeting, your perception will be that the water is not safe to drink, no matter what either of them tells you.

Some important things to remember about risk are that (1) the public is more willing to accept voluntary risk—skiing, smoking, for example— than they are to accept involuntary risk—polluted air, possible contaminated water; and (2) people look at risks differently. The government communicates in *macro* terms; the citizen thinks in *micro* terms. The citizen asks, "Can I drink the water?" The government official responds, "The potential risk from drinking this water is 10 to the minus 6, assuming a 20-year exposure to 5 parts per million of benzene contamination." The outcome is no communication.

Our advanced society has convinced many that it is possible to live a risk-free existence. But alar in apples, growth hormones in milk, and irradiated vegetables tell us that there is a price for living in our modern world.

Some argue that those who are exposed to more risk should be compensated. For example, in France, those who live near nuclear plants are entitled to free electricity. Some believe that tax abatement, recreational facilities, or jobs should be provided to compensate localities for the presence of prisons, garbage, pipelines, or waste sites.[21]

Communicators credit Professor Peter M. Sandman of Rutgers University for his pioneering work in describing the problems in communicating environmental risk to the public. Sandman notes that there are two issues—communicating with the media and communicating with the public.[22] From the media's perspective, he observes, environmental risk is not a big story. What's more important is what happened, how it happened, who's to blame, and what the authorities are doing. To quote an old journalistic proverb, "If it bleeds, it leads." Reporters also tend to focus more on the politics of an environmental issue than the science of it. It's easier to cover viewpoints than to try to sort out the truth.

Also, Sandman notes, risk in a story is simplified to a dichotomy: either something is hazardous or it's safe. There are no shades of gray. Further, reporters try to personalize stories to make them more interesting. Would you swim in that stream? is a lot more relevant to the media, and the public, than a report that benzene levels of one part per billion have been found in that stream and that the potential for cancer is $10^{-6}$. Finally, claims of risk are more interesting than claims of safety. To quote Kirk Douglas from an old movie, "Bad news sells best, because good news is no news."

The single biggest problem in communicating risk information to the public is that the risk-assessment process is so inadequate. Scientists normally use rat studies in which the animals are exposed to various dose levels and extrapolation is made to assess impact on humans.[23]

When covering environmental stories, TV news normally get their information either from citizen bystanders or government and corporate officials. Rarely does TV get information from experts or advocacy groups. [24]

Sandman likes to say that risk means more than annual mortality; it equals hazard plus outrage. The public, he says, pays little attention to hazard and officials pay no attention to outrage. Sandman's answer here is that officials should reframe the problem and make serious hazards more outrageous and modest ones less outrageous. Successful examples here have included campaigns against drunk driving and smoking.

A few of the main outrage factors include:

* Voluntariness—When people decide they want to do something, there is no outrage.
* Control—When people, instead of a government agency, are in charge, the risk—to them—is lower.
* Fairness—If people are going to accept more risk, the general consensus is that they should be compensated.
* Process—As we said before, the process is the message. If a process is honest, open, and credible, people will be less intimidated.
* Morality—People believe pollution is not only harmful; it's morally wrong. When officials talk about acceptable risk, that doesn't wash.
* Memorability—Once TV images like Bhopal or Love Canal get into the public consciousness, they are hard to forget.
* Dread—People have a greater fear of AIDS than of drinking, for example.

A number of guidelines can help an organization when these kinds of issues come up. One of the most important is to remember that most people worry about the hazard and forget exposure path. This simply means that they worry about the dangers of a chemical compound or waste, but don't always look at whether or not they are anywhere near where they will be exposed to the substance. You must have both to have a problem.

Here are some other things to remember:[25]

1. Help people understand risk. Quantify risks so that people can understand them: one part per billion equals a single crouton in a 500-ton salad.
2. Communicate widely, not just to the impacted cohort, but to the entire community.
3. Know the local situation. Connect with key community contacts who know the cast of characters and the issues.
4. Remember there are no dumb questions. It will take a lot of work, but you need to spend a lot of time educating as well as communicating. Most risk communicators fail to realize that if you take time to explain technical issues clearly, resistance will be less.
5. Remember Maslow's theory that people are driven by a hierarchy of needs, the most basic of which are survival and eco-

nomic well-being. Their concerns about risk are driven by these same needs.

6. Use language carefully. Don't use *mutant* when talking about genetic engineering, for example. Also, metaphors work especially well today in explaining technical terms.

7. Be preemptive with negative information. Don't let the other side release your negative information. Do it yourself and do it first. It will add credibility and let you put the right spin on the information.

8. Avoid dueling scientists. Try not to get in a situation where your scientist and the public-interest groups are fighting it out in public. You can't win in this type of situation.

9. Don't assume a lack of interest. Low meeting turnout has nothing to do with interest. Develop a program that reaches out to all impacted parties.

10. Be the good guys. Take the higher moral ground with environmental issues. Do the unexpected. It will add to your credibility.

An organization involved in a risk communication problem should: Get senior management involvement. The CEO is the most visible environmental symbol you have. If he or she is out front, then the rest of the organization will follow.

- Develop ways to stimulate dialogue on public concerns. Get management into situations where there can be a dialogue with public interest representatives that will lead to real resolution. Use the principled negotiation approach of Fisher and Ury's *Getting to Yes*.[26]

- Train company personnel. Set up a program in risk communications for technical staff so they can interface more effectively with the public.

- Promulgate successes. When something works, share it with others inside the organization, as well as with the general public. Success breeds success.

Finally, it's very important to build bridges in the community. Develop a dialogue through open houses, advisory panels, speakers bureaus, medical expert panels, plant tours, seminars, and hotlines. If people perceive you are credible and fair, they will give you the benefit of the doubt.

## THE WORLD IS GOING GREEN

U.S. businesses seeking to participate in the new world economy will find environmental concerns impacting their expansion into new markets. International incidents, such as the Union Carbide accident in Bhopal, the Chernobyl nuclear power plant disaster, and the oil well fires in Kuwait, along with widespread concerns over holes in the ozone layer, global warming, and deforestation of tropical rainforests, have resulted in an increasing number of conclaves by world leaders to get agreement on environmental cleanup and future world development.

Already, the Montreal Protocol on ozone depletion and the Basel convention on international shipment of hazardous waste have scored limited success in getting international cooperation. In addition, the Rio conference has achieved some limited successes on a broad number of world environmental issues including rain forests and global warming.

Nevertheless, large transnational problems remain as smaller countries seek to grow economically and large countries seek to slow pollution.

According to J. Andrew Schlickman, a senior partner specializing in international environmental law with the Chicago-based firm of Sidley & Austin, U.S. businesses seeking to expand overseas need to get a better handle on international environmental developments. Schlickman believes that international law will drive national environmental issues in many countries, that controls will be more market-based, and there will be more emphasis on criminal enforcement of environmental laws. His advice to business is to:

1. Monitor development issues closely.
2. Evaluate impacts of potential laws and treaties.
3. Become more active in international bodies that are deciding issues.
4. Become proactive through training of staff, auditing of facilities, and monitoring developments.


## SUMMARY

The Green Revolution illustrates how companies can do good, communicate their efforts, and reap success. No question that environmental compliance is difficult, especially for manufacturing and resource-extracting industries. But the evidence is becoming clear that the public will reward environmentally responsible companies and that the inevitable move towards sustainable development will create opportunities.

## ENDNOTES

1. John H. Sheridan, "Environmental Issues Sap Executive Time," *Industry Week*, March 16, 1992, pp. 44–48.
2. "The Greening of Corporate America," *Business Week*, April 23, 1990, p. 97.
3. Jerry Crimmins, "Environmentalism Surges in Poll," *Chicago Tribune*, July 9, 1991, p. 5.
4. *Ibid.*
5. Casey Bukro, "From Coercion to Cooperation," *Chicago Tribune*, September 17, 1991, Section 20, p. 6.
6. Quoted in "Briefings," *Public Relations Journal*, August 1991, pp. 6–7.
7. E. Bruce Harrison, "Plowing New Ground in Environmental Affairs," *Public Relations Journal*, April 1991, p. 32.
8. Paddy Carson, Loblaw's vice president for environmental affairs, quoted in Susan Schaefer Vandervoort, "Big 'Green Brother' Is Watching," *Public Relations Journal*, April 1991, pp. 14–19.
9. Adapted from Josh Baran, "Practical Tips for Dealing with Environmental Communications, quoted in Vandervoort, "A Big 'Green Brother' Is Watching," April 1991, p. 26.
10. "The Greening of Corporate America."
11. Kevin Maney, " 'Green' Labels Spark Push for FTC Rules," *USA Today*, July 22, 1991, p. 2B.
12. Stuart Elliott, "Advertising," *New York Times*, January 23, 1992, p. K.
13. Casey Bukro, "Shopping for an Ideal," *Chicago Tribune*, November 17, 1991, p. 20–24.
14. Mary Beth Sammons, "Crafting 'Green' Company Plan," *Crain's Chicago Business*, July 15, 1991, p. T1.
15. Bukro, "From Coercion to Cooperation."
16. Thomas Graf, "Industries Fail to Cut Toxic Wastes," *Denver Post*, August 27, 1989, p. B1.
17. Jonathan S. Naimon of the Washington-based Investor Responsibility Research Center, quoted in "The Nation's Polluters—Who Emits What, and Where," by John Holusha, *New York Times*, October 13, 1991, p. F10.

18. Richard C. Harwood, "Main Street America, Part I," *Western City*, September, 1991, pp. 6–60.
19. New Rules on Garbage Favor Large Companies and Huge Dumps," *New York Times*, January 6, 1991, p. C10.
20. Edward I. Koch, "A New Age of Feudalism," *New York Times*, December 26, 1989, p. 27.
21. Peter Passell, "Making a Risky Life Bearable: Better Data, Clearer Choices," *New York Times*, May 9, 1989, p. 1.
22. Peter Sandman, "Facing Public Outrage," *EPA Journal*, 1987.
23. Matthew L. Wald, "As Science Gauges Perils in Life, to Learn More Is to Know Less," *New York Times*, August 19, 1991, p. 1.
24. Michael R. Greenberg, Peter Sandman, et al. "Network Television News Coverage of Environmental Risks," *Environment*, March 1989, p.16.
25. "The Race to Manage Environmental Risk Is On," *Public Relations Journal*, August, 1991, pp. 6–7.
26. Roger Fisher and William Ury, *Getting to Yes* (New York: Penguin Books, 1983).

## Chapter Eight

# Communicating with External Audiences

Organizations have three main audiences—employees, customers, and society, or the public. Reaching outside the walls of the organization to communicate with external audiences that comprise society today is more pronounced than ever before.

The neat division of the sectors of society that characterized life in earlier times no longer exists. The public perceives that business, for example, is responsible for its impact on the economy of the nation, for the quality of its environment and public health, for the depletion of resources, for the quality of life in many U.S. communities, and even for some of the problems of national government.

Most businesses get involved in external affairs for defensive reasons:

- To ward off government action.
- To prevent growth of community animosity.
- To keep other interest groups, or even competing interests, at bay.
- To gain government help to develop markets.
- To make sure favorable—or at least nonthreatening—politicians are elected.
- To generally protect economic interests.

Any business organization that fails to get involved in external affairs will find itself at the mercy of outside forces. From a more positive perspective, organizations have gotten involved in external activities in order to develop a positive image that can build goodwill with customers. A lot of goodwill can be generated by a company helping kids stay in school, funding low-income housing, producing environmentally safe products, and giving 5 percent pretax donations to charity.

Many companies clearly see that if they do not get involved in certain activities, their future can be negatively impacted. For example, many companies have gone beyond simply supporting United Way and have, like Boeing Aircraft in Seattle, United Services Automobile Association in San Antonio, and other organizations, made strong commitments to mentoring and stay-in-school programs. These companies realize that dropouts take away from the labor pool and cost society money. This is good citizenship, but it is also known as enlightened self-interest.

The corporate communications department has many responsibilities in external affairs, and in this chapter we look at some of the most important of those responsibilities. In some organizations, these functions are not in communications. Instead where they are located doesn't matter, as long as the job gets done.

## THE FUNCTION OF MEDIA RELATIONS

What used to be called *press* relations meant dealing with the media. The original reason that a company had somebody in public relations was to keep the media at bay. But public relations people were not just there to keep the organization out of the media. They also had the responsibility of getting publicity, that is, serving as press agents. This activity helped defray advertising expenses by gaining free publicity in the news columns via publicity stunts and the like.

Good press could also help turn around a negative image. In the case of oil tycoon John D. Rockefeller, a famous robber baron, a press agent had him pass out dimes to children, with the cameras clicking, to demonstrate his generosity and turn around his negative image.

A little less than 100 years later, the same technique was being used by the New York public relations firm of Robinson, Lake & Palmer, which billed $150,000 a month in their efforts to clean up the image of a new robber baron, Mike Milken.[1]

Press agentry also extended to helping companies with products and technology. George Westinghouse is thought to be the first chief executive to use public relations, when he brought in two men to promote the use of alternating current over direct.

Reporters in the working press have, over the years, nicknamed public-relations people *flacks* and *shills*. *Flack* comes from *flack jacket*. The flack takes the shots from the media aimed at the company. A more recent term,

*spin doctor*, refers to the ability of a public relations person t
negative story and put a positive interpretation, or spin, on it. *Shil ___*
from the nickname of a person who touts up prices at an auction; the
public-relations *shill* touts up the company to the media.

The skills of a good media-relations person today include helping formulate a media communications strategy that supports many different
communications functions—from crisis management, to financial communications, to marketing of new products.

Good media-relations people develop and cultivate contacts in the news
business in order to just gain favorable news stories, and also to give
themselves insurance when bad news comes. The idea is that those news
contacts will at least call to get the company's reaction on a negative event.
The effective media-relations professional also understands how the media
works and helps prevent management from making mistakes, like failing
to return a call and thereby missing a deadline. Media-relations people can
help prepare management for interviews by finding out what the questions
will cover and helping prepare the manager. An extensive treatment of
this subject can be found in Chapter 9.

An important part of media relations today is crisis communications.
Crisis communications involves public-relations people as members of a
management team involved in responding to an event that impacts the
survival of the organization. The role of communications is to serve as
counsel to senior management and to make sure information gets out
promptly and empathetically to the public. Crisis communications (covered in greater detail in Chapter 10) is one of the most demanding areas
of corporate communications.

## ISSUES MANAGEMENT

To cope with today's difficult external environment, companies have had
to find a logical process for dealing with the impact of external forces.
Issues management—a process of identifying and tracking public concerns
in order to impact their outcome—developed in response to the efforts of
social cause groups in the past. Those groups showed how to succeed
by appealing to narrow interests, coalitions, the media, and government
agencies to mount campaigns to achieve goals such as passage of clean
water and bottle bill legislation. Environmental groups were especially
effective at identifying issues, developing coalitions, gaining news cover-

age and support of influential people, and achieving Congressional action in a well-coordinated and successful manner.

Legislation on drinking water, hazardous wastes, toxic substances, and water pollution steamrolled through Congress, backed by these groups and the coalitions of labor and others who had effectively mobilized grass roots support and public opinion.

The issues-management process is based on the premise that opinion precedes legislation, that trying to influence opinion early can be very important in controlling an issue, that such efforts should create credibility with employees and the public, and that when appropriate, alternatives can be put forward that will be considered to be in the public interest and not self-serving. Included in the process is the following sequence: (1) a problem arises; (2) it is identified and given a label; (3) a *hardening* process occurs, in which the issue becomes clearly fixed; (4) solutions are developed and presented; (5) the solutions often recommend legislation; (6) an implementation phase takes place; and (7) a new cycle begins.

Issues have been organized into three general categories:

1. Current issues—These are issues that are already being considered or acted on by government bodies. Bottle bills pending in various state legislatures are an example. At this stage, companies can only react to an issue, though sometimes changes in public and legislation perception of such issues can be affected either by companies or by external events in the society.

2. Emerging issues—These issues will probably be on the public agenda in the near future, but have not yet been formulated or hardened. Since the issues are in an evolutionary stage, this is an optional time for taking action to influence policy. Emerging issues have also been divided into three subcategories:

- Operational—those issues dealing with regulatory actions like product labeling, pollution, and safety.
- Corporate—issues such as plant-closing legislation, corporate takeover laws, and minimum wage.
- Societal—issues such as national health-care insurance, trade, and inflation.

3. Societal issues—Changes involving human attitudes and behavior fall into this category, and these issues are difficult to deal with. They include demographic changes, values, and lifestyle preferences.

The public-at-large usually does not initiate issues. Their great strength is passive—passive acceptance of pollution laws, or passive rejection of laws against drinking, as during the Prohibition era.

*Pressure groups* are the initiators and activators in issue formation. A small group can be as effective as a large group, depending on its ability to form coalitions, interest the media in its cause, and get support from political bodies. The role of the media is not to create issues but to spotlight them. Close monitoring of the media often helps determine whether involvement in an issue is warranted.

Because interest groups have become so expert at handling the media, issues can surface quickly in today's society. One need look no further than the soft-news shows like "Oprah Winfrey," and "Phil Donohue" to sort through a lexicon of today's hot topics.

Other ways to raise the volume on an issue is to attack other institutions such as business or government. The media, which today covers most news as if it were sports, loves to report on both sides and, if possible, raise the volume level. Politicians, who thrive on high-profile media coverage, also raise the noise level.

An elected official, however, is usually smart enough to see which way the wind is blowing before making a firm commitment. Considerations include the extent to which the legislator's constituency or committee is involved, the amount of pressure brought to bear by the interest group or an opposing group, and the legislator's ability to trade support on the issue with colleagues who have their own agendas. Also, campaign contributions weigh-in heavily.

The potential *impact* of an issue is also a concern. Some issues impact large segments of the public—equal rights, inflation, health care. Other issues, such as the deficit, the savings and loan bailout and capital gains, are more abstract to many people. Still other issues, such as civil rights and worker safety, are more narrow in impact and need strong leadership or events, such as the 1992 Los Angeles riots, to move them forward. Finally, there are technical issues, such as tax rules, tariff policy, and the like, which are remote for most people.[2]

## DEVELOPING AN ISSUES MANAGEMENT PROGRAM

A first step for corporate communications in installing an issues tracking and management system is to find out what is already being done. Is the strategic planning unit already doing environmental scanning? Is the legal staff monitoring the situation? Is the government relations office in Washington assessing legislative and regulatory initiatives? Is anybody pulling it all together?

Some external issues can have an impact on production, methods and costs, compensation and benefits policy, and accounting, to name a few areas. Some executives who think they know and understand the important issues facing their organization may have what is known as the home-office syndrome—the world begins and ends in New York or Washington, wherever home base is. Today a global perspective is needed in monitoring issues.

Methods for identifying issues are similar to those that have long been used in technology forecasting:

- *Intuitive forecasting*—expert opinion, Delphi studies, or structured polling.
- *Trend extrapolation*—plotting change three to five years in advance, based on a trend line.
- *Normative forecasting*—looking at established goals and outlining what efforts will be involved in achieving them.
- *Monitoring events*—environmental scanning of published and visual materials.
- *Cross-impact analysis*—studying the interaction of issues with each other and with other events.
- *Scenario building and modeling*—exploring implications of alternative actions and events.

The most widely used method involves scanning of published materials and public-opinion sampling. Communications departments in many corporations regularly monitor dozens of publications. Scanning also includes monitoring events in Washington—through trade associations or a local office—and monitoring via any of the hundreds of specialized newsletters that seek to point out trends.

Scanning is the intelligence gathering that underlies an issues-management operation. Studies show that most organizations do not formally scan on a regular basis. Reasons for this include continuing changes in top management, reliance on information from corporate outposts, lower budgets, and narrowly defined business perspectives.[3]

Once issues are identified, they need to be classified and categorized. The Conference Board has suggested a list of questions that can aid this process:

**FIGURE 8-1**
*The Issue Life Cycle*

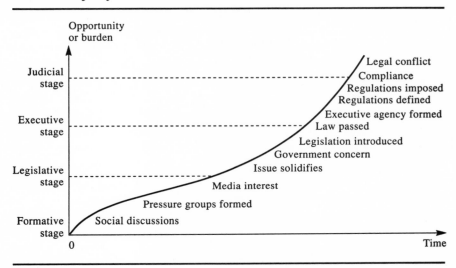

1. To what extent is the emerging issue due to internal, as opposed to external, factors?
2. From a detached, analytical perspective, what is the content of the issue?
3. Is it a *current* or an *emerging* issue?
4. What degree of impact is it likely to have on the organization? Is it going to be a public-policy issue or a strategic issue affecting financial well-being?
5. Will the issue affect the entire world or just a few corporations within an industry?[4]

Experts say that evaluation of an issue calls for a decision on what might be the worst-case impact on the company. Evaluation might be thought of as a present-value question: How much is preventing damage five years from now worth to the company today? This evaluation should be based on an assessment of potential impact on strategic areas: product lines, technologies, and geographic markets, and the relative profit contributions of each.[5]

It is easier for an organization to have an impact on an issue early in its life cycle than later. The longer intervention is delayed, the more difficult and costly it will become. Figure 8-1 shows this life cycle.

The next step in the process is planning what the company will do. Factors to consider include the *speed* at which the issue appears to be growing, and its potential future impact on the firm. Next, the organization must decide on a specific series of *actions* to take at various stages as the issue emerges. This planning should include top managers, operating managers, and corporate communications. Involvement at the highest level is required, since strategic interests are at stake.

In implementing a response, the task force moves to execute the agreed-on activity, which can include a wide range of actions: from doing nothing, to lobbying legislators, to coopting advocacy groups, to reformulating a product. The last step, program monitoring, entails measuring the effectiveness of the actions undertaken.

The real focus of this process is not on tactics but rather on developing recommendations as to whether the company needs to get involved, where the battle will be fought, and when it will be fought. Most advocates of the issues-management process stress the importance of developing a system that heads off trouble. This means the organization must work towards a monitoring process that can prevent surprise. The secret is in identifying weak signals in the environment. Examples of strategic issues that were preceded by weak signals were the invasion of Kuwait, the fall of Communism, and the savings and loan bailout.

### Governmental Relations

An issues-management action plan, as we have described above, often includes lobbying, dealing with regulatory agencies, and meeting with Congressional committee aides or administration appointees. In the past, many companies dealt with the federal government only through their local Congressional representative or through trade associations. In recent years, however, organizations have increased their presence in Washington.

The effectiveness of public-interest groups, like the Ralph Nader spin-offs, taught business the importance of being visible in Washington. Access to members of Congress through lobbyists and large campaign contributions via political-action committees (PACs) was supplemented with public-relations firms and lobbyists who developed the background information credible enough for Congressional representatives to use to argue in their behalf. Said one successful lobbyist and door opener: ''It's vital to be able to translate all that stuff into the language of politicians—into job, payrolls, and economic growth in a particular member's district. Then the member will listen to your case."[6]

When Ronald Reagan was elected president, some businesses trimmed back Washington offices because of a perception that government was going to get off the back of business, but most businesses continued to maintain a presence, some to take advantage in a time when government agencies' powers were being clipped by the Office of Management and Budget and various regulatory oversight panels.

In addition to collecting information on potential activities that may affect the corporate mission at both the government and international levels, the Washington office also feeds back data to many of these same sources, reflecting the company's position and reasons for its support of various bills, rules, or policies, For some companies, the Washington office also serves the business side by handling arrangements for selling goods or services to the government, keeping track of government requirements for new products, responding to government proposals, and sometimes working directly with operating parts of the company. The Washington office also handles the red tape and boiler plate often required for contracts.

The lobbying function is one of the most important that the Washington office performs. While the term *lobbying* has certain legal connotations, it is a loose word that can apply to anything from writing a letter, to providing information to a Congressional staffer, to testifying before a Congressional subcommittee. Washington insider Murray Weidenbaum divides lobbying with Congress into "offensive and "defensive" activities. The offensive posture is used to make sure the company's views on pending bills of special interest are known to senators, representatives, aides, and staffers. In the recent past, such efforts have been aimed at abolishing or at least amending the flood of federal regulatory legislation. The defensive function is geared toward stemming investigations or attacks on the company by providing immediate information to Congressional allies who attempt to refute any charges.[7]

Because of the high-level activities that the Washington office engages in and also because of its need to deal with company managers at many levels, the head of the Washington office is usually given rank of senior vice president. And while a Washington office can't be a complete substitute for the chief executive and can't handle many of the technical details involved in government operations, it can provide the connection point or the necessary access.

**Nurturing the grassroots.**   The realities of Congressional lobbying go beyond the task of providing information. They also require that an organization attempt to influence a member of Congress by fanning public opinion in his or her district—in other words, you need to communicate to the Congressman from two directions. Some companies use their own resources to orchestrate grassroots support; others use trade associations or public-relations firms. All use political action committees to funnel money into Congressional campaigns. Large trade associations such as the U.S. Chamber of Commerce, National Association of Manufacturers, and others run large-scale national lobbying efforts that can generate not only money but also thousands of letters when necessary.

Companies also use the services of large public-relations firms that orchestrate letter writing and media events such as rallies, news stories, and Congressional appearances. State-by-state campaigns to influence legislation are often costly and time-consuming, but certain industries, such as insurance, banking, and utilities, are significantly impacted by the power of the state.

**PACs.**   President John Kennedy once said that Americans had the best Congress that money could buy. How prophetic his words were. By November 1990, $440 million had been raised for Congressional races. A total of $147.8 million of that had been raised for incumbents by political action committees. Just $36 million had been raised for opponents. An astounding $28 million was given to candidates with no opponents. A former Kennedy speechwriter noted that there were no longer two political parties, but only one—The party of Washington.[8]

Originally, PACs were educational organizations set up by unions to funnel money to candidates. In the wake of the Watergate episode, Congress amended the federal election laws to limit the role of wealthy contributors and end secretive payoffs by corporations and unions by institutionalizing the PAC process. But instead of solving the problem, PACs *became* the problem. By the mid 1980s, there were thousands of them and the number was still growing. A PAC can give $5,000 to both a candidate's primary and general election campaign, whereas an individual can give only $1,000. Both, however, can give unlimited amounts to a political party, which can funnel the money to designated candidates, thus circumventing the law's intent. There are also ideological PACs that run campaigns on issues, such as environment, women's rights, balanced budgets, and so on. In addition, PACs have raised the cost of campaigning.

The continuing problem is that PAC money goes to incumbents, not to challengers. Bills to limit PACs have, expectedly, not fared well in Congress, though recognition of the problem is widespread. A number of activities including initiatives, recalls, and term limits have been used or tried to limit PAC influence. The issue of PACs is a moral and ethical one. For the long-term interest of the country, business should lead the move for reform.

**Trade associations.** Trade associations can be a very useful part of the organization's external communications activities in the area of government relations. Associations look out for members' interests by keeping them informed on government actions affecting particular industries. Associations develop positions on regulations and laws and represent their constituents with position papers and testimony before legislative, regulatory, and advisory bodies.

Trade groups also sponsor conferences and seminars to help members cope with laws and policies, once they are in place. Sometimes, trade groups go to court to fight for members. Such groups also undertake studies of the potential effect of laws and regulations and use that information for lobbying. Typical examples are the impact of compliance with clean air laws on jobs and the impact of foreign tariffs on grain sales.

In complex areas, such as occupational health or environmental regulation, trade associations can provide important advice and guidance to members who are too small to have the staff necessary to wade through federal regulations. Voluntary codes, such as the chemical industry's Responsible CARE program or the Hollywood movie-rating system can have a blunting effect on proposed government rules. Beyond trade associations, there are large umbrella groups like the U.S. Chamber of Commerce and the National Association of Manufacturers, which represent broad-scale business issues. The New York-based Conference Board and the Washington-based American Enterprise Institute provide business policy research that many businesses utilize.

The currency of trade associations, as with governmental relations offices, is *information*. Associations provide Congress with detailed analyses of proposed legislation unavailable elsewhere. This information often encompasses the consequences of proposed legislation in home districts of members of Congress.

## *International Intelligence*

With the end to the cold war in the early 1990s, the CIA discussed more broad-scaled international economic intelligence as part of its potential new mission. Such activities would mimic some of the routine economic and political intelligence-gathering already done by global corporations. International intelligence can come from a number of sources, including personnel stationed in foreign countries, a company's Washington office, and even staff assigned at the home office to collect this type of data.

It can be argued that political intelligence-gathering should be part of strategic planning rather than corporate communications. But it can also be argued that political intelligence-gathering is part of the issues-management process. A decision on placement within the organization should be based on how the firm is organized for gathering and processing information from outside sources. As the global economy expands and more and more Americans are stationed abroad, gathering this type of information should be easier. One of the reasons U.S. companies were so unsure of the Eastern European market in the early 1990s was due to a large part to the self-centeredness of U.S. society in general.

Various approaches have been developed for monitoring international risk. One model evaluates 10 variables for three periods: the present, 5 years out, and 10 years out. A second step involves giving additional weight to outside factors that might have an impact.[9]

## FINANCIAL COMMUNICATIONS

In the wake of the predatory era of corporate takeovers and consolidations, the role of financial communications seems to have become more difficult. In the recession of the early 1990s, the job of selling stock required extraordinary effort as debt-laden companies became unattractive. Only in rare situations during the last decade did communications play a significant part, and only in extraordinary defense situations such as that of Philips Petroleum.

More companies have begun using research to evaluate their image in the investment community. Certainly, stock price movement is a key indicator if investor relations (another term for financial communications activities) are working. Generally, it has been concluded that image advertising *does* help a company's stock price.

The job of the financial communicator is to clearly communicate the company's strategy, raise the level of awareness among investors, make top-level executives available regularly to analysts and the business media, and develop the print and electronic communications that provide information to potential buyers—large and small. The most notable communication produced by the financial communicator is the federally required *annual report*, a normally dull and trite publication that provides a historical perspective of the previous year—in pictures and financial summaries.

More importantly from a legal point of view, the financial communicator usually has the responsibility for following disclosure requirements for publicly traded companies under Securities and Exchange Commission (SEC) regulation.

The applicable policy is called *materiality*, which requires release of any information that can affect a company's profitability or financial position. Simply stated, the policy is, **WHEN IN DOUBT, DISCLOSE**. The major stock exchanges have published disclosure guidelines that emphasize:

- Immediately releasing any information that can materially affect the price of a company's stock: for example, the death of a top executive, merger negotiations that are complete, discovery of a new resource or process, imminent labor trouble, stock splits, gain or loss of a major contract, a major borrowing on the debt market, sale of a major asset, a tender offer for another company, or significant share sales.
- Quickly moving to stop unfounded rumors that affect a stock's price.
- Avoiding exaggeration—in other words, not making premature announcements or overly optimistic predictions, especially in news releases.
- Making sure everybody gets the same information at the same time.

Decisions regarding disclosure have to be made on a day-to-day basis and need the coordinated response of both legal and communications staffs. For releasing material information, Dow Jones and Reuters are two sanctioned wires in the United States which publicly traded firms can use to meet disclosure requirements.

**Box 8–1**
*Talking with the Financial Press*

When a senior manager meets with a financial reporter for an interview, it is wise to have the financial communicator present. Also, the interviewee should be prepared to use anecdotes and quotes so that his or her thoughts won't end up as background. It is important to be quoted. If the manager gets into an argument with a reporter, he or she might want to suggest some other source for the reporter to try, including some sources that might even disagree but are credible. Some experts recommend that interviews be conducted at the company's office, where file material is accessible. Some suggest that the interview be taped in order to have a record of what was said. New technologies allow senior executives to conduct video presentations to analysts right from their own offices.

A problem regarding quotes frequently may arise. If possible, get an agreement from the reporter to read back the quotes before printing or using the story. If the reporter is on a tight deadline, however, don't expect it. If the story appears and the manager feels wronged, the best approach is to write a letter to the editor, which will usually be published. It is important to be calm and set the record straight, especially by citing specifics.[10]

A company must be able to clearly and succinctly communicate where it is going and how it is going to get there. Strategy and vision communicated proactively is the centerpiece of financial communication. Investors are interested in the company's competitive position and market outlook, management's approach, strengths, and weaknesses.

Finally, studies note that after research, news articles and features about a company are the most influential factor in investor-buying decisions. Experts say it takes more time than money to do investor relations right—but you gotta be out there selling.

## CUSTOMER/CONSUMER RELATIONS

It has been said that companies love *customers*, but hate *consumers*. Customers buy goods; consumers complain. One of the hot buttons of U.S. business has been customer service. To some extent this has come about because of earlier consumer activism that resulted in stepped-up federal regulation of products and services. Safety recalls, contaminated foods, mislabeled products have all come under increased scrutiny through the years.

Many consumer product companies have long maintained good relations not only with their customers, but with consumer leaders and the general public:

1. *Customers*—An aggressive program goes beyond answering letters or dealing with problems as they arise. The program analyzes feedback and forwards it back to management, which incorporates it into decisions on design, manufacturing, and marketing.

2. *General public*—Opinion polls, consumer research, and surveys provide information on consumer desires and preferences that can often be worked into a company program. For example, consumer booklets on issues relating to gasoline use, which were distributed via magazines by Shell Oil, provided consumer information and product publicity at the same time.

3. *Consumer leaders*—Smart business people listen to what savvy consumer leaders have to say. Although consumer leaders are advocates, they are also well informed on consumer attitudes.[11]

Corporate communications people tend to be more involved in consumer relations than in customer relations, which is usually handled by marketing. However, when product announcements or recalls are made, the need for high visibility and rapid dissemination makes it urgent that media channels be used. (See Chapter 10, Crisis Communications, for a description of the role of communications in the Tylenol recall.)

## SUMMARY

An organization can create value by vigorous and continual communication with the many external audiences that make up society. A good image among the public not only makes achievement of the economic mission easier, but also provides some goodwill for a rainy day when things go wrong.

There are a number of jobs to do—media relations, issues management, government relations, grass roots public opinion, lobbying, international intelligence gathering, financial relations, and customer contact. Some functions will be handled by corporate communications; others by strategic planning, legal, government affairs, or marketing. What's important is not who's doing the job, but that somebody is doing the job and that it is coordinated inside the organization.

## ENDNOTES

1. James B. Stewart, *Den of Thieves* (New York: Simon and Schuster, 1991), p. 377.

2. Lloyd N. Newman, "Issue Management," *Public Affairs Manual*, National Association of Manufacturers, September 1980, pp. 2–3.

3. Charles Stubbart, "Are Environmental Scanning Units Effective? *Long Range Planning*, June 1982, pp. 139–45.

4. Robert H. Moore, "Scanning the Horizon for Emerging Issues," remarks to CNA Life Reinsurance Conference, September, 1978, Chicago.

5. Newman, "Issue Management," p. 3.

6. Walter Guzzardi, "How to Win in Washington," *Fortune*, March 27, 1978, p. 55.

7. Murray Weidenbaum, *Business, Government, and the Public* (Englewood Cliffs, N. J.: Prentice Hall, 1981), pp. 290–95.

8. George Mitrovich, "Public Funding for Elections, Money and the Politics of Betrayal," *Vital Speeches*, May 1, 1991, pp. 435–39.

9. F. T. Hammer, "Rating Investment Risk Abroad," *Business Horizons*, April 1979, pp. 17–23.

10. Reba White, "Coping with the Financial Reporter," *Financial Analyst Journal*, March–April 1978, pp. 38–40.

11. Camille Haney, "Business and Consumerism: Emerging Patterns of Partnership," *Columbia Journal of World Business*, Winter, 1978, p. 81.

## Chapter Nine

# Meeting the Press

In the wired world of the 1990s, credible communication with key audiences is a business necessity. A business or industry that fails to communicate its position or to respond to issues in the media can bring especially negative consequences on itself, including financial disaster.

When the apple industry delayed responding to a public interest group's attack, via "60 Minutes," for its use of the pesticide alar, harvest sales immediately plummeted. When Exxon ignored public reaction to the Valdez oil spill, it incurred regulatory wrath and heavy fines. Reluctance in the early 1990s by the health-care industry to take a stand on the high-profile issue of health insurance reform lessened its impact on the final outcome.

In the public sector, there is a tradition of disclosure of information, based on the idea that since the public pays the bills, it is entitled to know what the government is up to. In the case of the federal government, a powerful law, the Freedom of Information Act, governs the release of information and stipulates a bias towards disclosure. No such tradition or law applies to the business sector. Release of business information is governed by the Securities and Exchange Commission and the various stock exchanges and requires disclosure only of information that *materially* affects a company's economic condition. The goal is to ensure that everyone in the marketplace has equal access to information.

The tradition is that the private sector is private. Maximum disclosure, it is argued, would hurt competition. Reporters, usually trained in public-sector reporting—from police beats and the courts, to city, county, and state government—are used to operating in an environment where release of information is either routine or regularly demanded.

The sharp contrast in these two points of view was brought clearly into the open in 1991 when Proctor & Gamble, furious about leaks of what it considered proprietary information to a reporter from *The Wall Street Journal*, persuaded Cincinnati police to comb phone records of the city's 800,000 residents to find a culprit. Media reaction was predictably acerbic.[1] Proctor & Gamble's action was very consistent with its reputation for being highly secretive. However, as companies have come under greater government regulation and public scrutiny, they have found that a low profile can sometimes hurt their public image, turn opinion against their products, deflate stock prices, and do other economic harm. Salomon Brother's CEO John Gutfreund lost his job—and almost the company— by waiting four months to tell the SEC, and the world, that his traders had made improper bids on Treasury notes.

The need to communicate was not always a business imperative. But with new technologies like cable TV, new business publications, and expanding video channels, more opportunities to communicate have become available. In the 1980s, the story was the empowerment of business as a result of the "Reagan revolution" that had followed an era of oil shortages, civil rights concerns, environmental degradation and a new consumerism that had put business on the defensive. In the early 1990s, the story was that U.S. business was on the defensive, trying to get ready for a global marketplace, but it was financially weakened and faced an economic cold war with Japan and Germany.

To compete effectively in a new marketplace of public issues, such as regulation, trade, industrial policy, and the like, business has had to get involved with the media to reach the publics whose opinions drive national policy and political action. A company communicates via the media because it sees the economic utility of this action. It is a decision that must be made on the basis of economic impact.

Companies have few real requirements imposed on them to communicate. A privately held company has no legal obligation to talk with the media. Publicly held companies are still required only to communicate minimally to the public via annual SEC reporting requirements, such as 10(k) filings and annual reports, or when some action is being taken that might *materially* impact stock price.

But when a company desires government action, it must get out front and argue its case. It must find friends in the press, make its case to influential people and groups, and generate letters to Congress.

The media are normal channels for world-wide dissemination of information in U.S. society, but, at the same time, they are independent businesses and, collectively, a major institution: a *fourth* branch of government, as they have often been described. The media are also uniquely protected by the U.S. Constitution's Bill of Rights in carrying out their function of informing the public.

And while the media serve as a channel of information, by necessity, they abridge that information to fit time or space requirements imposed by their specific medium. This means that information gathered by the media is processed and filtered so that what is fed into the channel does not always emerge the same.

This power of the press to reach a vast audience with processed information is not to be underestimated. But with the eyes-open vulnerability of a Blanche duBois, those who deal with the media on a regular basis understand how often they are relying on the kindness of strangers to get their message out. Politicians and government bureaucrats have, over time come to understand and accept this power of the press and have learned to deal with it.

## BUSINESS AND THE PRESS: OLD ANTAGONISTS

Business managers, used to running a tight corporate ship, have a special fear of the media because they cannot control it A daily newspaper is not like an internal newsletter, where the sun always seems to shine. As a result, business people and the media have developed a cat-and-dog relationship.

There are many theories about the reasons why much hostility exists between business and the media. A few of those theories are listed in Table 9-1:

One study of the business-media conflict concluded: "To the businessman, too often the antagonism boils down to this—business builds up; the media tears down. To the media, too often the antagonism boils down to this—business always hides its wrongdoing; only the media penetrates this stone wall."[2]

A business organization can be most successful communicating in this difficult environment when it is *legitimate* and *credible*. A company is *legitimate* when it acknowledges its role in the economic and social well-being of the nation or world. It is *credible* when its words match its deeds (it's walkin' like it's talkin). Images take a long time to build and often there is some lag time involved—good deeds must precede a good image. So, while it takes time to build a reputation, it also takes time to destroy one.

But in today's media environment, Irving Shapiro's advice about not talking to the press (Chapter 2) seems to ring more true than ever as tabloid

**TABLE 9–1**
*Theories about Business-Media Hostility*

| Theory | Description |
|---|---|
| "I'm Boss" | Business people, especially senior managers, are used to having their way. "Just run it the way I sent it in, Sonny." |
| Reporters as labor | Reporters often view business people as labor views management, since most reporters are salaried employees of a large organization. |
| The business of business | Management believes its primary business responsibilities are to the shareholder and not to the public. |
| Too many bottom lines | Business often tries to hide bad news; the media concentrates too much on short-term information. |
| Two different worlds | Reporters need immediate access to high-level officials for comments on public/business issues. Corporate officials take their time. |
| Medium distortion | The media, especially television, are apt to try to show things visually—especially confrontations. Reasoned arguments are seldom as interesting. The media are perceived as concentrating on bad news. |
| Priorities | Business people judge news coverage by its effects—good or bad—on the business and assume that if the story is harmful, the reporter was out to get them. But reporters and editors judge a story on whether it will be interesting and significant, not by the impact on business. |

journalism rages on nightly television, as business recovers from the collective black eye it got for the greed and unethical behavior that characterized it in the recent past and for today's general economic malaise.

Two decades ago, the media started treating business more like a public institution as the public began realizing more and more the impact of business on their lives, what their kids watched on TV, their health, and their well-being. Business leaders were unprepared for this newfound attention and reacted slowly at first. The media, used to the give-and-take of dealing with government and politicians, found business people defensive and antagonistic, hidden behind their corporate spokespeople. Business people, on the other hand, discovered the media were very powerful, that they sometimes got things wrong, and that controversy sells.

By the time the 1980s arrived, business people had wised up and had gone to charm school. They had learned how to talk to reporters. They had brought in consultants and had gone through television training so that they could handle the treacherous terrain of the 6 o'clock newscast. They learned how to avoid jargon, how to be empathetic, and how to get their point of view across.

At the same time, the news media seemed to have been lulled into slumber. It missed one of the major business stories in U.S. history—the savings and loan debacle. Also, the media made heroes and gods of the Wall Street takeover artists who eventually were cited for the devastating impact of their deeds on the U.S. economy.

Today, the new and more difficult problems of a xenophobic U.S. society under economic siege seem to overwhelm the monumental geopolitical events of the day, such as the disintegration of the USSR and the economic rebirth of Europe and the Gulf War. The hypnotic impact of television and its potential for voyeurism attracted interest towards the sordid side of the news—the Thomas-Hill testimony, the William Smith rape trial, the Tyson rape trial, the election year slanders of 1992, and the seemingly unnecessary exposure of tennis great Arthur Ashe's AIDS infection by blood transfusion.

## THE PUBLIC AND THE MEDIA

The wariness with which business approaches its encounters with the media in many ways reflects how the general public perceives the media. A study by the *Los Angeles Times Mirror's* Center for People and the Press showed that public confidence in the media is in decline. The study hastened to add that people still "like the press because they like the news," but were concerned about such issues as bias and invasion of privacy of public people. The major gainer in credibility among the media were not newspapers, but CNN, which was perceived as giving news pretty straight.

Newspapers have been moving in the other direction—towards more interpretive reporting. Another concern expressed by the public interviewed for this study was that the emphasis on corporate profits of the major TV networks was influencing news coverage more than in the past. The study also showed that people have problems with the way the press has investigated the private lives of public figures.[3]

## THE HARSH NEWS ENVIRONMENT OF THE 1990s

The biggest problem of all for business, however, is that the environment of news dissemination is changing. Television has replaced print as the primary means of communication. Already, among people 25 and under, there is scant newspaper readership.[4] In 1991, Ted Turner was made *Time* magazine's man of the year because his Cable News Network (CNN) has become the world's standard in covering news in real time—as it happens.[5] (In the next chapter, we will deal with the implications of this on crisis communications.)

For business, there is greater access to the media because the number of channels, and thus opportunities, has multiplied. At the same time, the message is more diluted due to the greater number of information sources for readers, viewers, and listeners. Because of this proportioning of space and time and the propensities of the media, good news tends to reach a smaller audience, and bad news tends to reach a larger audience.

Television news has never pretended to provide more than just headlines, but the wild success of tabloid or reality television in the early 1990s edged network and local TV news coverage farther and farther away from any pretense to provide a serious alternative to newspapers or magazines. One TV tabloid, "A Current Affair," has higher ratings than the "CBS Evening News," according to A. C. Nielsen & Co. And according to its producers, the competing "Inside Edition" is the 10th most popular program on television.[6]

At the same time, there is a wide perception that the press is arrogant and not committed to truth. Ironically, during the 200th anniversary celebration of the Bill of Rights, one study showed that if Americans had to give up one of their freedoms to protect all the others, freedom of the press would be the first to be surrendered.[7]

The harsh environment of television news reporting is certainly not conducive to any in-depth understanding of business news. Here are some reasons:

- "High concept" and the length of soundbites—The number of seconds of an interview used in a TV news report—has been continually decreasing. As we noted in an earlier chapter, the length of soundbites has dropped significantly in the last 20 years. In some markets, the trend has been to get away from soundbites altogether and have the reporter summarize over pictures of the interviewee.

It is ironic that the treacherous wall of sound-byte journalism was first successfully breached in the 1992 presidential campaign by a businessman-turned-politician, Ross Perot. Perot's interactive, one-on-one strategy of communicating directly with the electorate via national call-in programs set the stage for a dramatic change in election campaigning.

Another result of the sound-byte mentality has been the era of "high-concept" news. Originally a Hollywood term, "high-concept" refers to a program or movie based on a simple, single idea that can easily be grasped in just a few seconds. For example, the Congressional check-cashing brouhaha was high concept and got tons of media but not much real impact, while the S&L crisis, a more complex story, got substantially less media attention, but had enormous real impact. Dramatic stories of human emotions and foibles get the coverage today: riots, earthquakes, the shuttle explosion—all are high concept.

- Tabloid TV news—This type of reporting plays to all of television's weaknesses as a medium by turning everything into highly emotional, simple stories that are often re-enactments of real events.
- The entertainment/news blur—The negative image that TV entertainment shows normally give business seems to carry over into news shows as the lines between news and entertainment programming continue to blur. One show, "I Witness," uses home video footage as its news source.
- The domination of pictures—Pictures, as we saw vividly during the Gulf War, drive the national political agenda. In an age in which everybody is getting the same information at the same time, the pictures drive public opinion, which in turn drives political leadership. This fact was made absolutely clear during the events that led to the rapid decline of the Communist state, the fall of Iraq, and the Los Angeles riots of 1992.

## THE POWER OF PICTURES

The power of television is its ability to use pictures—or be used by pictures—to define the national agenda. Leslee Stahl of CBS tells the story of a rather negative report she did on how the White House orchestrated television coverage. Her words ran behind pictures of President Reagan, talking with farmers, embracing athletes, speaking to veterans, and so on. When she received a call afterwards from the White House, she was shocked to hear the official remark, "Great piece."

"Didn't you hear what I said?" she replied.

He explained, "I heard what you said, but the American people didn't. When Ronald Reagan talks and when you run powerful pictures of him before flags and balloons and smiling children . . . the public doesn't hear you." "I knew it was true," she said.[8]

## MULTIPLE CHANNELS TO THE PUBLIC

Audiences are becoming more and more fragmented, and there is no longer a general public that is easily reachable. Even in local communities, the public consists of residents, employees, community activists, elected officials, and so on. For each audience, there are different media: for example, major television and cable networks for all audiences; regional newspapers, and radio or TV stations for local audiences; special media for minority and ethnic audiences; and special cable channels for business.

The good news for business is that there is a giant news hole. Because of budget cutbacks at news networks and stations around the country, it is estimated that at least half the news stories now run are developed by public-relations departments or firms.[9]

## REAL-TIME COMMUNICATIONS

The world is wired for communications like never before, and with it our conceptions of time and space are being redefined. Now, the entire world immediately knows of an event as soon as (if not while) it happens. And since bad news travels as fast as good news, companies and organizations must plan how to handle media in difficult situations. They no longer enjoy the information float of earlier times.

## PRINT VERSUS PICTURES

Newspapers tend to present a world view of events, stressing an information approach. In reporting on new OSHA regulations, for example, a newspaper reports the facts as presented by agencies, officials, and experts. Television, on the other hand, focuses on individual stories to convey information, possibly showing footage of the tragic 1991 chicken processing plant fire in

South Carolina, where violation of OSHA regulations resulted in the deaths of over 20 workers. One problem with television news is the diminishing attention span of viewers, which has produced continuous picture montages of three-second shots and simple headline reporting.

## IS THIS THE FUTURE?

Bill Moyers raised some serious questions about the state of the U.S. mind in society "where more people know George Bush hates broccoli than know that he ordered the Panama invasion, and more know Marla Maples than Vaclav Havel." Moyers quotes *Rolling Stone* magazine's conclusion that we are now in an era of "New News," where a new culture of information is evolving—"a heady concoction, part Hollywood film and TV, part pop music and pop art, mixed with popular culture and celebrity magazines, tabloid telecasts and home video." Is this what's seizing the country's social and political agenda?" he asks as he expresses concern for America's astonishing civic illiteracy.[10]

## DEVELOPING A MEDIA RELATIONS POLICY

Learning how to meet and communicate through the media is an *acquired* skill for most people. It is acquired on two levels: dealing with the media generally and dealing with television.

Before a company plunges into learning how to deal with the media, it ought to first make sure it has adequate policies and procedures for doing so.

Here are some considerations in developing a media policy:

- Should all media requests for information or interviews be funneled through the communications office?
- Is the organization decentralized so that calls can go directly to the affected operation? How should management be kept informed of inquiries?
- On what subjects and to what publications should the CEO, rather than a subordinate, speak?
- If there is going to be a spokesperson representing management, who will it be?
- How much authority to answer questions will that person be given?

A written policy should answer these questions and reflect the level of public involvement necessary to maintain the firm's position in the marketplace. A start-up company will most likely want a very aggressive, proactive media relations policy, whereas a Fortune 500 firm will most likely have a more conservative one.

Further, the policy should mesh realistically with public and press interest in the affairs of the organization. A company with few employees that sells primarily to business will tend to be of less interest to the media than one that employs thousands and sells to consumers.

The external communications policy should be responsive to the concerns of the media. Those concerns are usually quite simple: (1) when the media call, they want a prompt, authoritative response; (2) if reporters wish to speak to senior management, they should be able to do so, or at least they should be able to talk on the record with a spokesperson who represents the position of senior management on the issues at hand.

The policy should also spell out who handles what kinds of information. The communications director might handle general-information questions; the CEO, financial-information questions; and the product specialist, consumer issues.

The communications department should be responsible for tracking information requests and responses. If the CEO has just spent 10 minutes on the phone with *Barron's*, the nature of the questions and answers should be relayed to the communications staff so that what appears can be compared to what was said. If any new policy was iterated during the phone call, as sometimes happens, this can be shared with inside staff.

Emergencies and disasters (the subject of the next chapter) should be covered by special contingency plans, which may be quite different from the regular communications policy. Employees who could be involved in managing emergencies or disasters should be familiar with the criteria for changing from policy to plan.

If outside public relations counsel is to be involved on a regular basis, the communications policy should include this decision as well. If the call from *Barron's*, for instance, related to a takeover attempt on the company, the outside public relations firm involved should be routinely notified of such a contact and the nature of the interview.

Also, more than anything else, a good communications policy should reflect a positive corporate attitude regarding media relations. It should not be defensive or reflect an "us versus them" attitude. Instead the media should be viewed as a positive tool for representing the company's position externally.

Finally, the company should follow its communications policy. If a bank has touted to its employees and the press that it has a positive, open-communications policy and tries to hush up wrongdoing by senior management, that policy loses its value and so does corporate credibility.

## WHY PEOPLE LIKE THE NEWS

Business people, like all people, are first and foremost consumers of news. Why? Admittedly, there's a certain voyeurism and titillation involved (which certainly accounts for the popularity of TV tabloid shows such as "Inside Edition," "A Current Affair," or "Entertainment Tonight"). But, more importantly, people have a deep-seated need to confirm that their family is all right, their community is safe, and their nation is not in harm's way.

Over the years, researchers that go around the country trying to help TV stations improve their ratings have tested various stories on audiences. At times, they've used galvanic skin tests (which measure "sweat" rate) and laser pupilometers (which measure dilation). Their research has shown that stories such as **health**, the **economy**, **disaster**, and **crime** stories literally excite people's senses. The reason is that these stories play back to people's basic Maslovian concerns for security, safety, and shelter. Hence, people are most interested in "sensational" news.

When business people start contemplating communicating through the media, they tend to lose sight of the very reasons they themselves watch, listen, or read the news as consumers.

Most companies' reaction to dealing with the media is, "If we can't control it, let's keep away from it." A company like Proctor & Gamble spends upwards of $2 billion each year on television advertising. Why? For two reasons—to obtain an undistorted channel to its target audience, and to achieve a positive reception of that message. As long as you're selling Charmin, those goals are attainable. When you move into the arena of ideas and issues, TV is reluctant to let P & G promote lower trade barriers, for example.

## HANDS-ON WITH THE MEDIA

In dealing with the media, there are three broad strategies that today's manager might adopt when faced with negative news: (1) do nothing, (2) react only when something happens, or (3) be proactive.

The first and second options are often seen as conservative strategies, but today they might be considered risky. If an organization has bad news, seizing and releasing it before the media shapes the story often allows that organization to control how the story is played, or featured. But even with such proactive efforts, dealing with the media is more difficult now than ever.

## PREPARING FOR A MEDIA ENCOUNTER

In preparing for a media interview, one should be aware of the different types of media and reporters.

At the supposed head of the journalistic pyramid are the star reporters— the Mike Wallaces, the columnists, the first-string Washington reporters for the major general-circulation papers and weekly periodicals. In reality, this group is a mixed bag. Some of them, like Wallace, are certified tigers; others are pussycats. Washington reporters, as a group, pretty much go with the press releases. Local reporters in some cities and at some papers are very aggressive. Reporters in cities like Boston, Philadelphia, and Chicago have a tradition of aggressively pursuing stories. One should be aware of what the reporter's reach will be and get some background on that reporter before sitting down for an interview.

Also, there are substantial differences between dealing with TV and print. Since newspapers and magazines tend to have more space to convey complicated information, they are more receptive to it. The full script for a half-hour TV newscast covers less than half a page of type in the *New York Times*. Talking to print reporters is easier since it is likely that the reporter is a business specialist. But many CEOs will be much more worried about having to deal with a *Forbes* or *The Wall Street Journal* reporter than with somebody from a cable network. That's because of who's reading or viewing what's being said.

Consider the irony of the fact that a major daily newspaper might have a business staff of over 20 reporters devoted to business news, while a major New York-based TV network might have only 4 or 5.

## LOCAL VERSUS NATIONAL COVERAGE

Coverage in national press will usually be more informed than in the local press. A financial public-relations specialist at one Chicago bank said,

"You have to be very careful dealing with local reporters. It's a slow process; you have to walk them through it." With national press, it's much easier.

Another financial PR person added:

"It's a tough situation. Reporters don't know much about the company's business. They quote you out of context. They come in with a story idea and you have no idea what they're going to write. You're sticking your neck out in trying to cooperate. The problem with dealing with the press is that it's a nonwinner. You can take the point of view that anything said about you, pro or con, is putting your name before the public and therefore is going to be good for you. On the other hand, with the expenditure of time, it's worth absolutely nothing; they're just trying to get a story. I think the attitude around here is antipress. Not that we're against the press, but there doesn't seem to be anything they can write that we're really in favor of unless it's a glowing article and very accurate and those don't come around very often."[11]

There are four distinct phases in preparing for a media interview: attitude, advance preparation, execution, and critique.

**Attitude.**    It is important to realize that in an interview, especially a TV interview, the skills of the person asking the questions are probably sharper than those of the subject. The interviewer doesn't know more about the topic but most likely knows more about conducting interviews. You are on the interviewer's turf, even if the interview is in your office. Nevertheless, you should radiate enthusiasm for your subject and believe strongly in your point of view. Simply put, you must reflect the company's *credibility*.

**Advance preparation.**    It is important to prepare for a media interview. A smart manager, faced with an upcoming interview, will brainstorm with associates every possible tough question that might arise. This role-playing exercise is a moment for total candor on everyone's part. One associate should ask tough questions, while another times the response (if preparing for TV). Notes and documents are helpful when dealing with a print reporter, but at most, index cards should be used, and sparingly, for TV. The mock session should emphasize use of picture words and anecdotes that make key points. The best way to conduct the mock interviews is with a video tape recorder so that the subject and colleague can get a preview of how the interview and interviewee will look on the screen.

Another technique for preparing for an interview is to write down some very negative and uncomfortable things about the firm or its policies in one column on a sheet of paper, draft a list of favorable things in the other column, and then try to work out ways of bridging from one column to the next.

**Execution.**    In conducting an interview, many media experts stress appearance, especially for television. More importantly is the use of empathy. What you wear in your heart is more important. Never do an interview that is not from the point of view of the viewer or reader. This is a mistake that unions constantly make. The public is not interested in their members' problems, the public is interested in its own problems. The same goes for any organization communicating with the mass media.

A second key point in executing an interview is delivering key messages. Every statement that is prepared for delivery should have a key point to make— briefly and pictorially.

Key messages are high concept messages delivered in an easily understandable manner: "private schools can do a better job of teaching," "U.S. trade policy has no teeth," "we have an internationally famous hospital right in our hometown."

In developing key messages, remember there are strategic messages such as "Our job is to protect the public health and environment" (EPA) and there are tactical messages such as "Yogurt and 2% milk are among the many dairy choices for those trying to cut fat intake" (United Dairy Industries Association).

Know the key points that need to be delivered and make sure they lead your statement or dominate your answers.

When doing interviews for the written media, the subject of off-the-record comments frequently arises. The best advice is never to go off the record. But if you find it necessary, in order to put an action or policy into some sort of context, make sure the reporter you are dealing with has as much to lose from violating your confidence as you do. Never go off the record with a reporter you haven't worked with before.

Finally, and most importantly, tell the truth. Once the press catches a newsmaker lying, he or she puts a laser-lock on the newsmaker and will never forget that lie or let the readers or viewers forget it either.

**Critique.**    This is the final phase of the interview process. Today, it is easy to video or audiotape interviews for TV and radio. After an interview plays, evaluate it by asking associates to give their impressions of what went right and wrong. Then, decide what should be worked on for the next interview.

The question sometimes comes up, What happens if a reporter sticks it to you? There are many possible answers: write a letter to the editor, do a TV editorial reply, issue a clarification, and so on. If the story is still in play—if there are other editions or newscasts—try to get the reporter or editor to correct the mistake. Remember, just because you don't like the spin a reporter put on your story, there are only three real mistakes the reporter can make: he or she gets the facts wrong; he or she misquotes you; or the reporter takes what you said out of context.

Your two best approaches to this problem are (1) to refuse to deal with that reporter again, or (2) just let it go. This will keep a one-day story from becoming a two-day story.

## TYPICAL MEDIA ENCOUNTERS

There are several channels through which business people reach the media: telephone calls, interviews, news conferences, informal briefings, news releases, and query letters.

### *Telephone Calls*

Ninety percent of all interactions with the media are likely to be by telephone. Telephone calls are used, for example, when a reporter calls to ask for information, to confirm information, or to get a quote on how something affects your organization.

Here are the immediate steps you should take when you get a phone inquiry from the media:

1. *Find out what they want to know.* What does the reporter want to ask questions about? You are not obligated to take the call immediately, and you have a right to know what the subject is going to be.

2. *Get the right person to respond.* After finding out what the subject is, it's important to get the appropriate person to respond.

3. *Prepare for the encounter.* Work with a colleague who can play devil's advocate to quickly put together a possible list of questions and answers that might come up during the interview. Work out appropriate answers.

4. *Have key points to make.* Develop one or two key points you want to deliver. You're not doing the interview just to answer questions; you're trying to get a point across.

How long does this process take? It doesn't need to take more than about 15 minutes!

### Interviews

In these encounters, a reporter asks for a one-on-one interview—in person or on camera—for a story he or she is working on. If you decide to give the interview, the safest form is live television or radio because the interview will be conducted in real time, and the chances of your remarks being edited or misinterpreted are few.

### News Conferences

In these encounters, all media that cover the organization attend. A statement of about one minute or less is prepared and read by the organization's spokesperson. A news release, fact sheet, and visuals, if appropriate, are made available. By tradition, news conferences normally run about a half-hour.

### Informal Briefings

These encounters can be conducted for individuals or groups and may be in person or by phone. The purpose of the briefings is to explain or clarify certain points. Unless other ground rules are established, briefings should always be considered on-the-record. They are a good strategic approach to improving media relations and increasing the chances that when something happens, reporters will remember to call for a comment.

### News Releases

News releases are announcements written by the organization and distributed to the media. Releases that are mailed should be used only for routine stories like job appointments or promotions. Phoning or faxing a release or placing it on a wire service is necessary for major events, because releases that are mailed are often overlooked or misplaced.

### *Query Letters*

A query letter suggests an idea to the media outlet with the organization suggested as an example. Today, this is a very commonly used approach. The letter should be pithy—you have just a few sentences in which to "hook" the reporter's or editor's interest.

## MEDIA TIPS

Before meeting with the media, prepare thoroughly by knowing your subject. Figure out which questions are most likely to be asked and know the key points you want to make. You should have both a strategic message that explains your organization's mission and single overriding communications objectives (SOCOs) that spell out your organization's position on a specific issue. For example, the key SOCO for EPA is "Our job is to protect the public health and environment."

At the interview, answer questions in complete, easy-to-understand sentences, without using jargon. Speak clearly and adapt your material to the audience's interests. Use picture words, and if you are good at it, colorful phrases. Metaphors and analogies are very powerful communications tools. A good example was the U.S. president of Toyota, who, tired of being verbally beaten up every time he went to Washington, told the press he felt like the ad in the newspaper that read, "Lost Dog: missing one eye, has only three legs. Answers to the name 'Lucky.' " That comment clearly captured the sense of the U.S.-Japanese conflict on automobiles. Another classic was a new inspector general for the Pentagon appearing before a Senate confirmation committee. When asked about his integrity, he replied: "I never took as much as a cheese sandwhich off a contractor." Those are the kinds of lines that the media love and will quote directly— without any interpretation. Another important point is to identify what you say as fact or opinion.

Be positive in your responses. For example, if a reporter asks, "Why haven't you corrected this problem?" do not answer, "We haven't corrected this problem because. . . ." A better response is, "We've been moving as quickly as possible to obtain the necessary permits . . ." Make as many positive points as you can.

Tell the truth. Remember that an organization is only as believable as the people who represent it. Tell the truth because once caught in a lie, you will find it difficult to regain credibility, and years of positive image building can be seriously damaged. Do not speculate or guess an answer. If you do not know, say so. Then commit to getting the information as quickly as possible.

Do not go off the record with reporters unless they have as much to lose as you do if the agreement is violated. Also, avoid playing favorites among reporters. Giving one reporter a scoop can sometimes make enemies of many other reporters.

Before the interview, always practice with a devil's advocate. Practice with someone who can play the role of reporter. Have him ask the toughest questions and then work together to formulate answers. Also, practice making your points.

## MEDIA TRAPS

When going through an interview, there are various interview traps to be mindful of. Here are the most typical:

1. The set-up or presumption of guilt.

Example: "Considering the low regard people have for your industry, how do you expect people to believe you're not ripping them off?"

Solution: One solution is to break in politely and challenge the premise. (If you're on television, don't nod your head when these kinds of questions are being asked—viewers will think you agree with what is being said.) The second approach is to wait until the question is finished, then attack the preface: "What you have said is simply not true. Let's look at the figures."

2. The empty chair question purports to represent the views of a third party who is not present. Example: "Mr. Nadar has said that your product is a health hazard and should be recalled immediately." Or, "Congressman Jones says your industry needs more regulating."

Solution: You can respond simply, "I have not heard those remarks," or "I cannot believe the Congressman said that, but I believe the facts will show that. . . ." You should make sure not to attack someone who is not present.

3. The what-if question is speculative in nature.

Example: "What if gasoline goes up to two dollars a gallon?"

Solution: The best advice is to refuse to get involved in speculation and move to make your point. "I think that question is pure speculation. I think our real problem is conservation. . . ."

4. The interview trap of inconsistency refers to a question that points out unexplained changes in policy or action.

Example: "Your firm issued a press release previously, indicating that you would not leave this community and move to Mexico." Or, "You previously stated that there were absolutely no health problems associated with your new drug."

Solution: Clearly explain the reasons for the change, whether it was due to a change in policy or circumstances. For example, "Our intentions have always been to maintain a plant in this community. However, difficult economic conditions nationally and the flood of competing imports have forced us to consolidate operations." Or, "Until recently, our research indicated that our new drug had sufficient safeguards."

5. Saying, "No comment," is another interview trap.

Example: "Is it true your company is considering buying our local television station."

Solution: If you can't give a substantive answer, give a procedural one. Talk about the three Ps—policy, procedure, process. "We look at over 500 companies a year for possible acquisition. It is a major decision in every case and one in which there must be consensus in our company. We have not made a decision at this time concerning the local television station." You may not have given the answer, but you have given an answer.

## DOING TELEVISION INTERVIEWS

The lesson of the 1992 campaign was—whenever you get a chance, do live television or radio. You can't be edited, you get through to your audience directly and in an unedited manner, and when call-in questions are allowed, you get to dialogue directly, one-on-one with your audience.

• If possible, do your interview against a visual background. In a TV interview, especially, pictures are important. A famous example of this technique was the graphics used by Lee Iaocca in apologizing to the public on television for odometer tampering by some Chrysler executives. The chart simply stated that (1) tampering with odometers is wrong; (2) some Chrysler people have tampered with odometers; and (3) it won't happen again.

• Be focused and enthusiastic. A 30-second television news soundbite is considered lengthy, but it hardly leaves time for in-depth explanations.

Open the interview with a brief summary of your key point, and express your point of view enthusiastically.

* Never assume the recorder is turned off. Anytime a camera or microphone is near, consider yourself on stage and act and speak accordingly. Any number of times each year a person in the news forgets that the microphone is on. In late 1991, for example, Nebraska Senator Bob Kerry told an off-color joke to a running mate while the C-Span microphone was open.

* Speak to and look directly at the reporter not at the camera. And remember to address your remarks with the viewer in mind.

* Dress conservatively. Blue or gray suits are good choices. Avoid shiny jewelry or loud-patterned clothing. Tinted-lens eyeglasses help to cut lighting glare.

* Know the program. Watch a few broadcasts of the program or newscast before your interview. Observe the style of the interviewers, anchors, and reporters, and get a sense for how much time those being interviewed are allotted to respond to questions and to support their answers. Again, remember, the safest medium is live television or radio. They can't edit your remarks.

* Relax. Although you are not a television professional, and might have butterflies and sweaty palms, remember that you have something newsworthy to say. Do some breathing exercises just before you start. Visualize success.

## DOING RADIO INTERVIEWS

Interviews on radio are easier than interviews on television because there are no lights or cameras, and you have more time to make your points. Here are several points to help you with a radio interview:

1. Work from notecards. Have facts and examples on notecards that you can quickly flip to when making your points.

2. Know your audience. Who is listening (e.g., male, female, young, old, educated, low income)? Tailor your messages to their interests and concerns.

3. Be conversational and brief. You may also want to repeat or rephrase a question, especially if it comes from a listener over an open telephone line.

4. Assume you are always on the air. When you enter the studio or take a phone call from the radio station, assume anything you say is being broadcast.

## SOME SPECIAL PROBLEMS

**Handling misquotes.**   When the media misquotes you, writing a letter to the editor or demanding an editorial retraction does not usually receive much attention. The best strategy is to call the reporter's editor and complain, but be specific. Remember, just because you don't like the spin, or way in which the story was presented, doesn't mean you have a case. Limit your concerns to misquotes and misstatements of fact. Complaining won't make it right, but it might prevent others from being made and, in a situation where there are multiple deadlines, you may be able to correct the story for the next newscast or edition. Remember the following five tips:

1. Use a written statement.
2. Take your time answering questions.
3. Stick to the facts; don't ramble.
4. If you don't know an answer, say so.
5. Assume everything you say will be quoted.

**Discussing technical issues.**   Scientific and technical discourse requires establishing a premise, presenting arguments, and reaching a qualified conclusion. But reporters usually want the conclusion first (i.e., before or without the facts that support it). Significant conflicts occur when technical experts try to communicate research findings or technical information to the media. They can only urge the reporter to wait for the explanation that supports their key point. One way to work through this process is to use the fax to transmit a quick, written response to the reporter's question. This serves the need of the reporter for a prompt response and the technical person's need for precision.

## BUSINESS, THE MEDIA, AND THE LAW

In 1964, when the U.S. Supreme Court ruled in *New York Times v. Sullivan* that virtually anybody in the news was a public figure and would have to prove malicious intent to win a libel case, the media hailed the decision as a major step forward in protecting freedom of the press. That protection has sometimes held firm and sometimes caved in, but generally it has held firm. And while plaintiffs often win at the trial level, the media more often win on appeal.

Business people have often felt compelled to go after the media in court as Mobil Oil did with the *Washington Post* and *The Wall Street Journal* in the late 1970s. Few of these suits are successful. One major success was a multi-million dollar award against CBS by Lorillard, the tobacco company, after a commentator at the network's Chicago station contended that the company was trying to get teens interested in smoking.

A number of public opinion polls conducted in conjunction with the 200th anniversary of the Bill of Rights have generally shown a great unhappiness by the U.S. public with the media. But as of yet, the impact has not been felt in the courts.

## SUMMARY

By virtue of the impact of business on U.S. society, today's communications environment, and the way business is conducted, managers must develop strong skills in managing the news media relations. Today, there is no place to hide.

Today's media environment is more hostile than ever, but managers can be successful if they know what their key messages are, carefully select the appropriate medium, and practice ahead of time. Managers can avoid media traps by working ahead of time with a devil's advocate. Managers should understand, also, that they can take certain steps to avoid getting misquoted and that if they are wronged by the media, there is recourse. Live radio and television is always preferable.

## ENDNOTES

1. Alan Farnham, "Biggest Business Goofs of 1991," *Fortune*, January 13, 1992, pp. 78–83.
2. Howard Simons and Joseph A. Califano, Jr., *The Media and Business* (New York: Vintage Books, 1979), p. ix.

3. Thomas B. Rosentiel, "Public Confidence in the Press Dips Sharply, Surveys Find," *Los Angeles Times*, November 16, 1989, p. 1A.

4. David Shaw, "Luring the Young, for Papers, Generation Is Missing," *Los Angeles Times*, March 15,1989, p. 1.

5. "Prince of the Global Village," *Time*, January 6, 1992, p. 20.

6. Sharon Bernstein, "Tabloids Continued Success—With the Viewers," *Los Angeles Times*, August 11, 1991, p. 7.

7. Tony Mauro, "Bad News for a Free Press," *USA Today*, November 6, 1991, p. 13A.

8. Stephen Bates, *If No News, Send Rumors, Anecdotes of American Journalism* (New York: Henry Holt and Company, 1989), pp. 23–24.

9. Jube Shiver, Jr., "PR Boom Isn't Drum-Beating, Public Relations Industry Expands Beyond Publicity," *Los Angeles Times*, March 24, 1985, p. 1.

10. Bill Moyers, "Old News and the New Civil War," *New York Times*, March 22, 1992, p. E15.

11. Frank M. Corrado, *Media for Managers* (New Jersey: Prentice Hall, 1984), p. 93.

## Chapter Ten

# Crisis Communications

When technology redefined time and space, crisis communications became important.

The story is told that it took almost two weeks for the news to reach Paris about the outcome of the Battle of Waterloo. Contrast to the real-time world of the 1990s—when world leaders get information faster from Cable Network News (CNN) than from their own staffs, where the world is instantly in touch with field commanders running a war, or where a little girl who falls down a well immediately has the prayers of many millions.

At the same time, the ability of organizations to react to crisis has not necessarily kept up. Organizations, like normal people, go through predictable stages when crisis appears: denial, isolation, anger, bargaining for time, depression, grief, acceptance, acknowledgment. An organization that has not prepared, trained, or practiced for potential crises will not be able to react effectively in the real-time communications environment it will face.

A need for crisis communications techniques was realized as a result of the confusion, rumors, and botched communications that were the hallmarks of the near meltdown of the Three-Mile Island nuclear power plant in the late 1970s. The hard lesson learned from that episode was that an organization should inform the public as quickly and completely as possible about a damaging occurrence in order to calm nerves, stop rumors, and restore confidence.

Some companies seemed to have learned from Three-Mile Island's experience. Johnson & Johnson's response to the Tylenol poisonings and Union Carbide's initial response to the Bhopal disaster are two oft-cited examples. But Exxon's response to the Valdez incident was a testament to the short memory of others.

Most organizations have to be dragged kicking and screaming into crisis planning. Most crisis planning in organizations begins *after* a serious crisis has already taken place. While studies have shown that most major companies have some sort of crisis planning in place, many middle-size firms still do not.[1]

One need only look at the headlines to see situations in which companies and their top execs have botched the communications during a crisis situation. AT&T senior management was almost invisible when the system went down in the New York area, disrupting air traffic. Source Perrier pretended there was no problem when benzene was reported in its pure waters. Drexel Burnham Lambert decided to go out of business rather than respond in a timely fashion to its credibility problems. Dow Corning closed its silicone breast implant business in the wake of a scandal involving the suppression of internal health studies. Even one of America's legendary consumer companies, Sears, found itself the subject of strong public criticism and lost sales for its slow response to charges by the states of California and Connecticut that it was pushing unnecessary repairs on its auto store customers.

Crises are messy, and they don't necessarily end quickly. Major disasters like explosions, plane crashes, and accidents involving human lives continue in the courts, in the press, in the public's collective memory, and in the lives of those involved. The television images of the John F. Kennedy assassination live on as part of the visual landscape of America's memory.

Also, the public demand for information and greater media awareness of the complexity of crises has boosted disaster coverage. In Kansas City, for example, the *Star* hired its own architects and engineers to determine the cause of the walkway disaster that killed over 100 people during a tea dance in the 1970s.

Formerly, most companies caught in a crisis situation attempted to maintain a low profile, and they were generally successful. An airline public relations man once related that years ago his first responsibility after a crash was to paint out the airline's name at the crash site.[2] Today, when an accident like the explosion of the *Challenger* takes place, it's out there on CNN television network for everybody to see.

## THE LESSONS OF THREE-MILE ISLAND AND TYLENOL

The lessons that came out of the accident at the Three-Mile Island nuclear power plant (TMI) near Harrisburg in March of 1979 and the Tylenol poisonings in Chicago in 1982 have often been cited as baseline cases in the study of crisis communications, and for good reason. TMI clearly showed the truly negative results that can come from botching communications during a crisis situation, just as the managing of the Tylenol episode showed how good planning and common sense can really be effective.

Before TMI, nobody really thought much about the importance of having crisis communications procedures spelled out in advance. But the mistakes made by Pennsylvania-based Metropolitan Edison during the crisis were so significant that lessons were quickly drawn. The first mistake was that the company did not tell it all. Reporters covering the accident had, for the most part, little understanding of the process, but they quickly figured out that the company wasn't delivering credible information, especially when the head of engineering, in a briefing to the media, omitted the fact that radioactive water had been discharged.

The TMI incident showed that business managers often fear reporters' bias and ignorance to such an extent that they refuse, or agree only reluctantly, to talk with the press. When they *do* talk, they are so steeped in jargon and qualifications that existing communications gaps are only exacerbated.

On the other hand, when reproters get conflicting or confusing information, or see that a person is dancing around the issue, they immediately become suspicious. ''All an organization achieves by ducking questions,'' said one public relations executive, ''is to assure its point of view will not be presented or that someone else is going to present it—someone who doesn't have its best interests at heart.''[3]

Once Metropolitan Edison was caught trying to hide information, the media quickly turned on it. Also, the company that had designed the plant refused to talk to the media. In the wake of confusing and inadequate information, rumors began to circulate, and as many as 100,000 people began to flee the area.[4] The day was finally saved when President Jimmy Carter sent in Harold Denton, a soft-spoken Southerner with a soft voice and candid style. Described as disarmingly frank and reassuring, Denton took charge of the situation and calmed the populace and the media.

At Johnson & Johnson (J & J), the first act of CEO James Burke, when he heard reports that cyanide-laced capsules of Tylenol were killing people in Chicago, was to fly a scientist, a security specialist, and a public relations person to Chicago to get firsthand information. Fast action was the mark of J & J. Plants were checked to make sure the poisonings did not result from any part of the manufacturing process.

Next, the company began public-opinion polling to find out how the public was reacting to the crisis. J & J learned that 94 percent of the public knew that Tylenol was involved in the poisonings, but 87 percent realized that the Tylenol was not responsible for the deaths. The bad news was that 50 percent of the public said they would no longer buy Tylenol products. A week later, armed with what information it could gather, J & J made two tough decisions: it recalled 31 million bottles with a retail value over $100 million, and it announced a reward of $100,000 for information leading to the arrest and conviction of the responsible party.

Based on continued polling, the company realized it could save the product and decided to maintain the product while introducing a new tamper-resistant packaging. As a matter of fact, new packaging was eventually introduced for thousands of consumer products as a result of the Tylenol episode. Within months, the company regained almost all the customers it lost. Why was J & J so successful in managing its crisis?

Johnson and Johnson was successful for several reasons. One reason is the company's corporate vision. Long before corporate vision and values were in vogue, J & J held regular meetings to discuss corporate beliefs. The text for those management meetings was a credo written by Robert Woods Johnson, the founder of J & J, that spelled out the company's commitment to its customers and their health. CEO Burke believed it was this commitment to the public that gave the company the determination to take the bold actions it did to recall and relaunch the product.

Another reason for J & J's success was smart marketing. Just weeks after the crisis ended, the company flooded the market with 40 million discount coupons at the time when people returned to the stores to get refills of competing products that had moved in following the recall of Tylenol. J & J offered retailers a 25 percent discount for ordering supplies in the same amounts as before the recall.

The company also used good press relations. The once nearly invisible (from the media's point of view) J & J management did a complete about-face once the crisis hit, seeking out national exposure on major news and talk shows, while its small public relations staff handled thousands of media inquiries and other employees fielded 35,000 consumer calls on a toll-free hot line. Looking back at what happened, Burke remarked, "We've gotten strength from this, not weakness."[5]

## MANAGING CRISIS

Two issues are involved in any crisis situation: *anticipation* and *reaction*. A company can develop approaches for anticipating crises in a number of ways.

Companies that fall short in anticipating crises, also tend to fall short in terms of their ability to react to crises. The mere existence of a plan is by no means a guarantee that such a plan will be executed effectively. For example, Exxon had a crisis communications plan, as did Alyeska Pipeline before the Valdez accident. AT&T had a disaster plan and backup systems when AT&T's batteries ran out and shut down air traffic in New York in 1991. The fact is that no matter how good a job communicators do, a myriad of problems can often complicate the situation: timing, management timidity, legal interference, political opportunism, and so on. In the midst of a crisis, fatigue, anxiety, and other forms of emotional stress appear and compound the situation. Judgment blurs, people are tired, they don't think straight, and mistakes are made.

There are rules and precepts that need to be followed in crisis management and communications, but none is more important than the one cardinal rule of "TELL IT ALL; TELL IT FAST." Information that gets out quickly stops  rumors and calms nerves. A continuing flow of information indicates that somebody is working on the problem. When information is not quickly forthcoming, a void is created that some other source will fill, and companies may quickly find that they have lost control of the story. One rule for crisis communications is to speak from one platform.

In a crisis, it is better for *one* person, rather than six, to describe the event. If too many people are telling different stories, the media tends to get the story wrong and no one appears to be in charge. For example, in the hours following the Reagan assassination attempt in 1981, the public was confused as to who was running the U.S. government. (Remember the famous Alexander Haig remark, "I am in charge"?)

If two sides are competing to be the credible source, public confidence will be shaken. This provides a strong argument for crisis communications planning between public and private organizations. The Chemical Manufacturers Association developed Responsible Care™/CAER (Community Awareness and Emergency Response) so that in the event of an accident, local public safety agencies and nearby residents would work together and not compete. Title III of the Superfund Amendments and Reauthorization

Act of 1986 (SARA) mandated this type of emergency-planning activity in a community where hazardous substances are located.

A frequent question that arises is, Who should the spokesperson be? Should it be the top executive, a communications spokesperson, or a responsible on-scene official? The answer is "all of the above, depending on the type of crisis. For an accident, the key spokesperson should be the communications person, with some help from technical specialists if necessary. For crises higher on the intensity scale, such as those relating to public health and safety issues, major financial problems, or where the financial markets or top government officials are involved, it may be necessary for the CEO to be the spokesperson.

The one-platform, approach, however, means that all responses are coordinated. This is especially important in a situation where a number of people from within the company are enlisted to communicate to various groups— such as customers, employees, shareholders, and a large cohort of media. In these situations, it is important that everyone work from the same script—the same statement, the same worked-out sheet of potential questions and answers.

The one-platform rule doesn't always work well in practice, however, especially when a crisis takes place far away from company headquarters, where plant personnel or the office manager has not been trained in crisis management, is relying on written guidelines alone, and may not have any procedures worked out with local public-safety officials.

One other issue to consider with the single-platform approach is whether or not to hold a large-scale news conference. The media feeding frenzy that took place during the Three-Mile Island nuclear power plant accident made companies wary of the large news conference format. The strategy employed by Johnson & Johnson during the Tylenol crisis was to hold a video newsconference simultaneously with reporters from major cities, and to have a staff available to respond to telephone inquiries. This approach provided a safe and effective substitute for the large-scale news conference approach.

## KEY PUBLIC MESSAGES IN A CRISIS

Someone once said that in a crisis, the public wants to know only two things: Who messed up? and What are they doing about it? Actually, the public wants to hear several things:

---

**Box 10–7**
*When the Heat's On*

Be accessible but get your act together first.

Corral the press. Set up a single information dissemination point.

Centralize information release. Establish a single spokesperson and location.

Anticipate questions. Don't answer questions "on the fly."

Spotlight heroes. Focus on positives.

Cooperate with other organizations involved.

Stay "on the record." There most likely will be a lot of reporters you haven't dealt with before.

Don't withhold information. If and when it gets out, you'll lose all credibility.

Have your video and facts on file. Control the picture and information.

Get to the media that count, such as wire services and networks.

Be pre-emptive. Release your own bad news first and you'll control the story.

---

1. "We're sorry"—This simple phrase, which has worked for millennia in healing human wounds, tends to strike fear in the hearts of litigation-minded attorneys, who fight communicators' efforts to deliver this message. The litigator's argument is simple—the phrase implies admission of wrongdoing. But in at least one state, Massachusetts, the law will not allow an expression of sorrow to be used against a company in a civil case.[6]

2. "We're taking action"—The public has a right to know, especially in crises that impact public health and safety, that something is being done. The more specific you can be, the more at ease the public will be.

3. "We're doing it quickly"—Another question the public wants answered is When will the crisis be over? You may not be able to tell them exactly, but by explaining what you're doing and how fast you're doing it, they may be able to infer how long the crisis will continue. One thing to be careful of here, however, is never to get involved in setting deadlines that might not be met. In the wake of the devastation of the oil fields in Kuwait, the firefighters brought in from the United States were very conservative in their estimates of how long it would take to put out almost

**FIGURE 10–1**

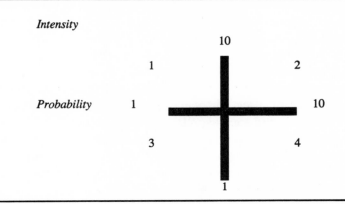

a thousand fires. When they finished well ahead of plans, they looked a lot better than if they had missed their estimates.

4. "Here's how you can help"—Americans have a long tradition of rolling up their sleeves and pitching in when help is needed. The public will go out of its way to be helpful, to do what they can when they're asked. This goes for the media as well, especially when public health and safety are involved. Use that goodwill when you need to.

5. "We care"—When Union Carbide chairman Warren M. Anderson got on a plane and went to India in the aftermath of the Bhopal accident, many criticized the action as cosmetic. But the lack of such symbolic action on the part of Exxon in the wake of the Valdez disaster drew the most criticism. Union Carbide also provided $1.8 million in disaster relief, suspended production of Methyl isocynanate gas, and did not try to pin the blame on its subsidiary.[7] Too many times, the lawyers get in the way with the result that the message "We care" never gets delivered.

## MAKE EVERYTHING POSSIBLE PUBLIC

The less people know about what is going on in a crisis, the more they fear possible consequences. The national hysteria that followed the Arab oil embargo, the Chilean grape recall, and the use of the pesticide alar on apples brought home the fact that when there is no information available in a crisis, rumors breed quickly.

It is important not to hold back any information during a crisis situation. This is part of the "tell it all" rule. This means telling all pertinent details, as long as security or confidentiality is not breached. Following an incident or accident, the media will want to know the usual information—who, what, when, where, why, and how. A smart company quickly provides straightforward answers to those questions.

At the same time, many questions require speculation concerning cost or damage, specific causes, and blame. These questions should be deferred with a simple response such as, "It's too early to tell," "We just don't know at this time," or "We can't speculate on that." When information is available, however, it should be shared. United Airlines was criticized for holding back passenger manifests from the public after the Sioux City, Iowa, crash of a DC-10 in 1989.[8]

## UPDATE THE SITUATION CONTINUALLY

When a situation is fluid, frequent updates of information are important. In a crisis situation, information overload is appropriate. As we mentioned above, when there is little or no information available, rumors develop. Frequent accounting builds trust and confidence. Lapses in the flow of information stimulate speculation and increase anxiety.

## PLANNING FOR CRISIS

A crisis can be an accident or emergency that poses a major threat to the survival of an organization. An accident is a dramatic, disastrous event, such as a toxic chemical leak or an explosion or an airline crash. An emergency is less dramatic, but can have equally traumatic consequences, such as an official who absconds with funds or a labor action or a radically changed market. Two criteria apply equally to both situations: (1) how close the crisis could come to closing down the organization, that is, the intensity, and (2) what the likelihood or probability is that it will happen. (See Figure 10-1.) A rigorous program of crisis management involves developing, testing, and updating crisis plans on a continuing basis.

If an oil company is evaluating a possible explosion at a refinery, it might plot intensity or impact on the company as very high, especially if it was a gasoline refinery. Such an accident could produce a consumer shortage as well as seriously impact profits. In addition, if the accident happened in a period of high oil prices, the financial impact could be very high. Therefore, intensity could be significant, say at five or six, at least for the short term. Sometimes, the impact can go on significantly longer: the Bhopal accident forced a major long-term restructuring of Union Carbide. The DC-10 accident in Chicago in 1979 that killed almost 300 people, some say, eventually doomed the airplane, which is no longer manufactured.

The second factor, probability, is sometimes more difficult to evaluate, though actuarial statistics provide some guide. If we study the relation of the two, we find that crises with high intensity—rank in quadrants one and two—seem to provide the greater threat to the organization. Our conclusion is that the primary concern in evaluating potential crises is the perceived intensity level.

## FIVE BASIC STEPS OF CRISIS PLANNING

The five key steps in the process of developing a crisis communications program are shown in Figure 10–2.

### *Developing Internal Support*

Crisis planning normally gets underway the day after a crisis has taken place. Chalk this up to a flaw of human nature that seeks out the good and blocks out the downside. But often it takes a real crisis to get the attention of senior management focused on the subject.

How do you get top management's attention focused *before* a crisis occurs? Frankly, it's not easy. One study a number of years ago showed that about 42 percent of companies that had gone through a crisis still didn't have a plan after the crisis had passed!

While every organization has its own culture and values and quirks, there are some steps that can be taken to get the ball rolling. First, realize that there must be a champion who will devote his or her energy to breaking through the inertia. That champion can come from anywhere on the management team. The champion's job is to energize the process, to make the case for crisis planning, and to take a "show" on the road inside the organization to sell the benefits. The most vexing problems will be the political ones: Whose support do you need to get others to support it? Who

**FIGURE 10–2**
*Five-Step Crisis Planning Process*

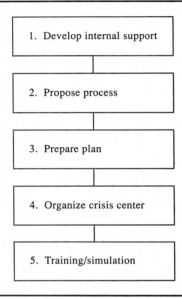

will fight or support it no matter what? The first step is to find an ally and brainstorm with him or her for a strategy to sell the idea.

The crisis team is usually constituted into three groups:

1. Top executives—Those who will actually manage a crisis. This group is usually made up of the CEO and other senior managers, regional and field management.

2. Support group—This group normally includes technical specialists, quality assurance and risk managers, human resource management, and environmental affairs directors.

3. Communications—These are top communication managers and technical specialists. Their job is to facilitate communication between the team and the outside world.

Once the players have been identified, the next step is to prepare a briefing or road show that can be presented to each. The presentation can be a simple series of overheads or flip charts. There are several key points to make.

**Today's communications environment.** In any presentation to senior management, it is important to point out how interconnected the world is today. A couple of the examples already cited should suffice. Talk about crises that similar organizations have faced in the recent past.

**Types of crises that could happen.** Crisis must be defined broadly. It needs to be noted that there are many different kinds of events that fall into the category. A fairly broad definition would cover a number of types:

- Public health and safety—the Bhopal disaster; Love Canal; the Kansas City Hyatt walkway collapse; the Imperial Foods fire that killed 25 workers in North Carolina; the Chicago underground water leak that temporarily shut the city's business district.

- Legal and political troubles—the savings and loan debacle; the Salomon Brothers' bond-trading scandal.

- Customer relations—the Kraft minivan giveaway crisis; the AT&T shutdowns in the Northeast.

- Labor—Eastern Airlines; the air controllers union and Ronald Reagan; the 1991–92 Caterpillar strike.

- Product failure—the Perrier contamination episode; the milk contamination at Jewel Foods in Chicago; the Rely Tampon; the Firestone 500 radial tire.

- Management continuity—the plane crash that killed Dell computer's management team; the death of Robert Maxwell.

- Takeover battle—the RJR Nabisco battle; Philips Petroleum; and a host of others in the 1980s.

- Changed environment—industrywide downsizings during the 1991 recession; IBM's place in the computer industry; the banking industry after the savings & loan crisis.

- Money problems—Bank of Boston's money laundering;Chrysler's loan guarantees.

- International events—U.S. companies that sold high technology to Iraq; trade problems with Japan.

The presentation to management should include going through the above list and then spending time brainstorming other possible kinds of crisis that could specifically impact your organization. This should be an interactive process. Before the presentation is made, a Delphi study might be conducted with the top managers. The study should include a list of questions on possible types of crises that might face the organization, with each manager ranking the five most likely to occur. The presentation could focus on crises most often identified by their peers. Have each manager plot his or her crisis picks on the scale shown in Figure 10–1, which shows the relationship between intensity and probability.

**Readiness of the organization.**   In selling the idea of crisis planning to top management, important questions to ask include: How well can we detect a crisis early? How well could we manage a crisis? Do we have a system in place to handle a crisis before, during, or after it happens? and How well does negative information move upward? For most organizations, thorough self-appraisals and honest answers to such questions will underscore the importance of crisis-management planning.

**Outline a plan.**   The presentation should spell out the various steps involved in a crisis-planning process, so that managers have a clear understanding of how the process works, what the time commitments are, and what outcomes can be expected.

## Proposing a Process

Once the need for crisis planning has been accepted, a crisis-planning process should be proposed that will include representatives from all levels of the organization: key executives, including the CEO; communicators; and staff (e.g., legal, claims and risk, human resource, and technical specialists). The crisis champion should work with the CEO to map out who will be on the team, what will be covered in the plan, when the group will have its first meeting, and other details.

## Preparing a Plan

In formulating a crisis plan, the crisis team lays out procedures for notification and response. The team clarifies who will do what, and when. The team also specifies who will inform employees and the public and what methods will be used to do so. A one page policy statement, usually written by senior management and prefacing the plan, is an important indicator of how committed the company is to risk reduction and crisis management.

The policy statement also expresses the organization's philosophy on how it responds to its needs as well as to those of the public.

But planning does not end with the plan; it is an ongoing process of continually weighing information, developing strategies for a range of potential crises, and periodically testing the organization's ability to respond to them.

## *Organizing a Crisis Center*

A crisis center is simply not a room filled with alarms and blinking red lights; it is more likely to be a simple in-box and a calendar, or a room that is activated and staffed when needed. Whoever is in charge of staffing the crisis program is usually also responsible for the internal and external monitoring that uncovers danger signs and puts the crisis team into action when the crisis occurs.

When it meets, the crisis team has a number of responsibilities. Among them are:

1. Assessing possible threats on a regular basis.
2. Developing and testing possible crisis scenarios.
3. Investigating internal problems that might lead to a crisis.
4. Preparing simulations and tests of the crisis plan.
5. Organizing internal and external resources that might be called upon in a crisis situation.

## *Conducting Training and Simulations*

The most important role a crisis team plans is that of remaining alert to potential crises, conducting brainstorming sessions to come up with strategies for managing them, and offering media training and simulations to test and implement crisis procedures.

It is important to note that crisis responses will vary depending on the type of situation. The response to a labor crisis is not the same as to a product-reliability problem. That is why the crisis team needs to keep reviewing potential crisis situations, developing strategies, and adding to the plan.

The Federal Emergency Management Agency has established classes of crisis simulation exercises. The three most relevant include:

- Tabletop exercise—This is informal, familiarization training. Sitting around a table, participants talk through the exercise. This involves low stress. The exercise can be "frozen" at any point and a discussion held concerning problems raised. This exercise is sometimes held as a preliminary to a field-simulation exercise.
- Functional exercise—At this level, a group actually goes through some or all of the actions that would be required of participants in an actual emergency situation. The purpose of the simulation is to test the planning and response capabilities of people and systems without actually doing the real thing.
- Full-scale exercise—In a full-system test, an actual incident is staged, involving all personnel and logistics. This is a very expensive activity and involves disruption of actual business operations and involvement of large numbers of people.

Usually, a crisis team spends time doing table-top walk-throughs of various crisis scenarios. At least once or twice a year, however, a simulation should be conducted for the most likely scenarios. Depending on the organization's activity, a full-system test may be warranted. Chemical plants, airports, and large manufacturing/processing plants are examples of facilities that should occasionally conduct full-system tests.

The purpose of simulations is not only to help fine-tune the crisis plan, but also to provide realistic training to crisis team participants.

## CAN WE PREDICT CRISES?

A subset of crisis management ripe for research is that of evaluating previous major organizational catastrophes for weak signals that may have given some indication crises were coming. Most people involved in crisis management believe that there is a time before a crisis happens when the potential for trouble can be detected. Many feel this was the case with the Bhopal and Chernobyl accidents. Studies of air crashes often show that the problem could have been detected ahead of time. This does not mean that it's possible to anticipate crises in every instance, but certainly, looking for those early signals is worthwhile.

A whole body of helpful technology forecasting tools is available. We've already touched on one of them—the Delphi study, which harnesses the collective judgment of the organization's best minds to try to make some educated guesses about what might happen. (Missing here sometimes, though, are the people far enough down in the organization to really know what's going on.)

Another tool is trend extrapolation. If you sell jeans and your market is getting older each year and you miss that point, you may have a product crisis like Levi Strauss & Co. did in the early 1980s. Simple trend extrapolation can sometimes predict a problem.

The tool of expert opinion is based upon what top people in your industry say is going on that might cause a crisis and the kind of research that is going on at the universities that might give you some warning.

Finally, there is scenario development. One of the most important things a crisis team can do is sit around and speculate "what ifs." This kind of brainstorming can have enormous benefit uncovering the unexpected. One of the major burger chains asked for help in developing its crisis communications plan. Its primary concern was food contamination. The first question back was, What if a major civil rights or educational leader called for a product boycott based on claims of exploitation of child labor, low wages, or unhealthy food? What if a mass killer started shooting people in one of the restaurants? They had never thought of that.

Another major help to the crisis management team can be provided through the issues management process. Using various monitoring techniques, a group can evaluate what public issues, which might affect the organization, are moving from social discussion to political action to regulation or legal action. (See Chapter 8.) Environmental concern, women's rights, the backlash to civil rights, and the cultural diversity movement all moved through this process. Trade issues, population shifts, and support for labor can all be monitored in terms of their impact on U.S. public opinion. As we mentioned earlier, a sea change may be coming in U.S. politics as a result of the current perceived economic decline of the United States. This is the kind of issue that could have enormous potential crisis impact for certain kinds of businesses and should be closely monitored. Advertising researchers have done an excellent job of measuring psychographics of U.S. consumers to help with marketing. Now, it is important to harness this research capability for crisis management as well.

## COMMUNICATORS VERSUS LAWYERS

One of the major problems senior management must deal with in a crisis situation is conflicting advice from staff, especially communicators and attorneys. Lawyers are trained to think in terms of liability and of protecting their clients. One public relations counselor, James Horton, suggests that in a crisis, lawyers see torts at every turn. This thinking often translates into advice to management to hunker down and say nothing (since anything it says might be used against the company).[9]

A public relations professional, on the other hand, is trained to find out who, what, where, when, why, and how to report that information. Essentially, public relations people are interested in image and reputation; attorneys are interested in protection. Different as these two viewpoints are, however, they share a common goal: what is best for the organization. On that common ground, they need to be forced to develop a strategy that will both enhance and protect.

"Public relations professionals and attorneys can benefit from each other's knowledge during a crisis," observes Richard Hyde, a New York-based senior vice president at Hill & Knowlton with extensive crisis management experience. Hyde recommends working out relationships in advance of a crisis. "Mutual respect and cooperation are hard to learn in the heat of crisis," he says. When relationships are not worked out in advance, top management is left to make the decision, and the downside view often presented by legal counsel tends to prevail.

For example, Robert B. Irvine, who runs a national crisis management database, stated that during the early part of the Exxon Valdez incident, he and a team of crisis experts made recommendations to help repair the image of the Aleyaska Pipeline Company, which had been severely damaged because of poor response time in getting the cleanup going. The attorneys prevailed upon senior management to do nothing, with arguments like, Are you willing to risk criminal indictment? "It's an unfair fight," says Irving. He contends that attorneys often tell management, "You can listen to the PR people and you'll look good in the press, but you'll probably be indicted on criminal charges. Or you can listen to us, keep your head down, and you'll be let off."[10]

## CRISIS ADVICE FOR SENIOR MANAGERS

Here are several suggestions for successful crisis planning.

1. *Insist on early planning*. With worldwide communications operating on a real-time basis, an organization has no time to hash out how to disclose

news of a damaging occurrence; it must be prepared to act immediately and decisively.

2. *Set ground rules*. Management should insist that the crisis team develop ground rules and procedures on how quickly information will be released, what internal tracking mechanisms will be used before releasing information, and what the role of legal counsel will be. Before a crisis, decisions need to be made on who will be informed, and in what order: employees, shareholders, local community, national media. Decisions also need to be made on who will advise management about its options.

3. *Do not underestimate the effect of negative publicity*. The court of public opinion meets before the court of law and can have a significant impact later as individual and class-action cases come to trial. If there is a media laser-fix on poor corporate performance, the story will be hashed as each case comes forward. And the impact could have political and regulatory repercussions and eventually damage the organization's bottom line.

Management must be willing to buy the argument that going public to calm public concerns and assuage public outrage might very well be the most protective action of all. My argument is this: you are going to court either way. You'll have a better chance with public opinion on your side.

4. *Think in visual terms*. Pictures drive the national agenda in the United States as we have said earlier. How is this crisis going to look on the 6 o'clock news? That's a key question that any crisis-planning effort must think through. Having file video footage available in advance for the media may help negative visual impact. Think through in advance what you are willing to show.

Some final advice for CEOs is quoted here from Gerald C. Meyers, the former chairman of AMC Corp., who went on to become a crisis management expert:

Misfortune is manageable, but there are rules for executives: Take charge or take it on the chin. Don't follow your first impulse to minimize the problem. Assume the worst so you will extend yourself to your maximum capacity. Don't wait for the facts; there probably won't be many. Head for the scene to assess the damage. Draw conclusions and act fast. Ducking the blame will derail your recovery. Be the source of bad news, not the victim of it. Don't hesitate if you're forced to choose between helping people or saving money.[11]

## MANAGING CONFRONTATIONAL CRISES

It would not be surprising if the 1990s saw a rebirth of social activism of earlier times—in labor, in community and social rights, and in other areas. We have seen a strong growth of social activism in the environmental movement starting in the late 1980s and continuing in the 1990s.

This type of crisis is characterized by well-organized, media-saavy groups that are adept at political manipulation. Greenpeace, the national Right-to-Life Federation, and others have learned that power is rarely bestowed and almost always taken forcefully.

Here are some basic rules regarding confrontation, which were developed some time ago by Allstate Insurance after the company faced community charges of redlining:

1. *Confrontation is a means to an end.* That end is negotiation and change. The faster one moves to discussions, the less hassle one has from the media. The cost of not meeting with a group is higher: in morale, productivity, and energy needed to keep fighting, plus damage to the company's image. Decisions to meet and negotiate with groups need to be made early.

2. *Not all groups want discussion.* Attacking groups sometimes just want a *target*. They want to posture, and do not really represent a constituency. You might decide to meet with groups that are broadbased and honestly looking for solutions. When you have to refuse, leave the door open for the future.

3. *Management must be trained to deal with confrontation.* You may be facing some really angry people. You need executives trained in managing hostile situations. Often, a sorting process needs to be used to choose those managers for training who have the temperment for this kind of interaction. The sales department is a good place to look.

4. *Rhetoric must be ignored.* In *Getting to Yes*, an excellent book on negotiations, Fisher and Ury point out that in negotiating you must separate people from the problem. Also, some groups need a visible, procedural victory more than they need a substantive one. It's important to get past the words and determine what the other side really wants.[12]

## SUMMARY

The world is now wired together in real time. This means that when a company stumbles and falls, everybody in the world can immediately know about it. For this reason, crisis communication is now more important than ever. Crises that impact public health and safety require immediate and concentrated actions, as do those that directly impact consumers.

Companies that fail the public will end up hurting themselves financially. There are five key steps that any organization can use to introduce a crisis planning process. The most important of those is selling the idea to senior management. The key rule of crisis communications is—Tell It All, Tell It Fast. Companies that do this and show empathy will do best in the long run.

## ENDNOTES

1. A University of Southern California survey of the nation's largest industrial companies found that only 38 percent of 114 respondents had a formal crisis team. A similar study by Western Union showed that about half of 200 respondents had a crisis communications plan. See Nancy Jeffrey, "Preparing for the Worst: First Set Up Plans to Help Deal with Corporate Crises," *The Wall Street Journal*, December 7, 1987, p. 23.

2. Thomas Petzinger, Jr., "When Disaster Comes, Public-Relations Men Won't Be Far Behind," *The Wall Street Journal*, August 23, 1979, p. 1.

3. Micheal L. Drohlich, "Manage PR Crises through Advance Planning," *Scope*, May 1980, pp. 7–11.

4. Casey Bukro, "How Accurate Was Press about Three-Mile Island?", *Chicago Tribune*, March 30, 1980, p. 2–1.

5. See Michael Walkholz, "Tylenol Regains Most of No. 1 Market Share, Amazing Doomsayers," *The Wall Street Journal*, December 24, 1982, p. 1; Thomas Moore, "The Fight to Save Tylenol," *Fortune*, November 29, 1982, pp. 44–49; Michael Waldholz and Dennis Kneale, "Tylenol's Maker Tries to Regain Good Image in Wake of Tragedy," *The Wall Street Journal*, October 8, 1982, p. 1; and Michael Millenson, "J & J /Gains Admiration, Strength," *Chicago Tribune*, November 21, 1982, p. 5–1.

6. In Massachusetts, the law has been amended to allow organizations to say, "We're sorry," without fear that such statements can be used against them in a civil action. "Statements, writings, or other benevolent gestures expressing sympathy or a general sense of benevolence relating to the pain or suffering or death of a person involved in an accident and made to such person or to the family of such person shall be inadmissible as evidence of an admission of liability in a civil action." See *Massachusetts General Laws*, chapter 133, Par. 23D, 1986.

7. Edward Rouse, "Union Carbide Comes to Grips with Its Image Problems." *Philadelphia Inqurier*, December 14, 1984, PD 01.

8. Carol Jouzaitis, "Crisis Response by United Gets Passing Grade," *Chicago Tribune*, July 23, 1989, sec. 7, p. 1.

9. Frank Corrado, "Environmental Crisis Management: Attorneys and Communications Professionals Working Together, *Environmental Law Reporter*, March 1991, pp. 10115–10118.

10. *Ibid*.

11. Gerald C. Meyers, "A.T.&T.'s Bad Connections, *New York Times*, September 29, 1992, p. F13.

12. Quoted in *Media for Managers*, by Frank M. Corrado (New Jersey: Prentice-Hall, 1984), p. 114.

*Appendix A*

# Government and the Nonprofit Communication

Over one third of America's gross national product (GNP) is spent by government at the state, federal, and local levels. And if you add expenditures on private education, health-care delivery, plus association and not-for-profit activities, the sum equals one half of the country's goods and services.

Communication activities play a larger role in the public and nonprofit sector than in business.

## GOVERNMENT AND COMMUNICATION

On the way to the year 2000, government is rethinking the way it does business, and in some cases, it is reinventing itself. It really doesn't have much choice. Governments at all levels in the United States are in serious trouble.

The high-flying 1980s redistributed wealth at the upper end of society and left a poorer middle class to try to fund services for the increasing numbers at the lowest end. The average family of four in the early 1990s paid $3,000 a year in federal taxes, just on interest, before it received anything back from government.[1] The problems facing government include declining revenues and built-in spending increases in areas such as health care, education, and public safety.

At the same time, bureaucratic organization, which has been the mainstay of public management for the last century, is suffering a breakdown in areas like social welfare. Hence, the inevitable negative news stories of abused children being returned to unfit parents, welfare being cut off to the truly needy, municipal cutbacks in garbage collection and police and fire protection, and generally poor delivery of services continue to give government a bad name.

Voters have made a strong case, via polls and at the polls, that they want better government for the money they are paying. As David Osborne writes in his book, *Reinventing Government: How the Entrepreneurial Spirit Is Transforming the Public Sector*, taxpayers say they want governments that are less bureaucratic and more entrepreneurial.

When you think about it, local government represents a large captive market bound economically to a good-sized piece of real estate. A wide variety of businesses want access to that market and will pay for it, via franchise fees. Waste haulers are happy to pay for the right to collect garbage and make a profit. A municipality can provide developers and employers with investment incentives to encourage renewal and economic development. These approaches are an attractive alternate to a government monopoly that breeds inefficiency.

Many governmental units are experimenting with a range of new approaches, such as:

- Putting greater emphasis on use of parent- and community-run facilities like schools and public housing.
- Using creative management structures to get around government rules.
- Establishing service levels instead of line-item budgets, and rewarding managers who exceed those levels.
- Providing those on assistance with vouchers so that users can have a choice, thus forcing landlords, job trainers, day-care centers, and others to compete.
- Using the new technologies to decentralize and push responsibility to the lowest level.
- Becoming more market-oriented, via economic incentives to control pollution (for example, bottle deposits and transferable air pollution credits).[2]

This more entrepreneurial, market-driven approach will require stronger marketing and communication from local government. It will mean decentralizing some of the political power as well.

## MARKETING GOVERNMENT SERVICES

The potential for government marketing derives from the benefits provided by government as well as the marketability of the service. Some services that are not very marketable, include fire and police protection, clean water, and adequate sewage service. *Marketable* services include disease prevention; fire safety; vehicle inspection; housing; public transit; pollution abatement and environmental preservation; industrial development; and quality schools, libraries, and museums. Criteria include such factors as voluntary use by citizens, availability of public-market alternatives, cost-effectiveness, and social merit.[3]

Certain things government does, or provides, are marketable—fire prevention, which is not the same as fire protection. So, by emphasizing fire prevention, government is really trying to cut the use of fire protection services.

The Connecticut Department of Transportation used marketing successfully when it introduced a weekday commuter train service to bring East Shore residents into New Haven to work, and to connect with other trains. The purpose of the train was to stem choking increases of traffic. The strategy was to generate trial ridership and reach average usage of 400 riders per day. The approach was to offer the first month of service free, using coupons, and gaining high-media visibility. A half year later, paid ridership had reached 550 per day.[4]

Direct marketing and public relations by the bi-state Kansas City Area Development Council attracted over 250 new employers to the area. Community leaders undertook the marketing effort after it was determined that the area was not capitalizing on the new awareness created by a new airport and dual sports stadiums.[5]

The federal government, through the National Institutes of Health and other agencies, is spending billions of dollars to try to halt the use of drugs among young people, and it is spending millions more to market the idea of safe sex.

A major question about government programs that advocate behavior changes in the population is simply, Do they work? For example, in the mid-1970s the federal government spent $5.8 million on a national effort to increase public awareness of high blood pressure and to reduce the number of people in the United States who had it. Statistics showed that during the same five-year period, the rate of deaths due to strokes decreased by 18 percent, twice the rate of the previous five-year period.

In addition, a 50 percent increase was observed in roughly the same period in the number of visits to physicians for hypertension-related reasons. There appeared to be a correlation between the national public information/education program and the reduction in strokes and visits to doctors, but no formal evaluation was conducted.[6]

National advocacy programs to get people to stop smoking, prevent forest fires, stay in school, and the like are even more difficult to assess. One of the problems is that most government agencies don't or can't advertise. In light of our previous remarks about the diminishing importance of advertising in the marketing mix (see Chapter 6), one might conclude that advertising is less credible than public information/education, so it doesn't matter. Actually, there's probably an anomaly here: government information/education programs tend to start off with more credibility because of the source. Advertising might actually make them more effective because the message would reach more people. Questions regarding the efficacy of public service versus paid advertising, cost-effectiveness of a marketing approach, and other variables have not been adequately researched, though millions of dollars are spent annually. One of the classic examples was the many millions of dollars in free ad time urging urban residents to help Smokey prevent forest fires.

Studies by the Congress General Accounting Office have shown that for information and education programs to succeed, every government marketing campaign has to include four elements:

1. Objectives. Information campaigns should have clear objectives that can be achieved at a reasonable cost. Meaningful objectives are also important in determining program success.

2. Audience targeting. The more precisely the intended audience is identified, the more closely the specific messages will be based on audience knowledge, attitudes, behavior, and media habits.

3. Information channels. Dealing with complex issues that may require a change in attitude or behavior (littering, smoking, safe sex) often requires a mix of information channels including media, community elements, professional organizations, and interpersonal contact (with high-profile role models, for example).

4. Evaluation. Evaluating the effectiveness of information dissemination can be difficult, especially when such factors as economics, personal attitudes, and behavior are involved. Nevertheless, it is important from the outset to establish clearly how information dissemination can be evaluated. Such evaluations can take many forms—from measuring distribution of information materials to conducting complex studies of behavior changes.[7]

# COMMUNICATIONS MANAGEMENT IN GOVERNMENT AGENCIES

*Internal* communications in government agencies has in the past often mimicked that of the private sector. The differences seem to be that job security rules in the bureaucracy tend to inhibit good management and this often results in an authoritarian model, where communication happens mostly via the grapevine.

In terms of *external* communications, government is generally viewed as belonging to the taxpayer, and there is a tradition that encourages vigorous media coverage of governmental activities.

A sustaining interest by the media in the affairs of government has kept the glare of public exposure on the actions of government. The affairs of local, state, and federal government have been covered with increasing sophistication throughout the years. Government is a traditional and abundant hunting ground for investigative reporters, and stories on government corruption are regular grist for newscasts.

The coverage given to governmental affairs is substantial, though it tends to concentrate on politics, which is easier and more like sports coverage to a media that likes to cover the news by reporting points of view. Coverage of the workings of the bureaucracy is often dependent on the public relations announcements of agency heads or political chieftains: the governor announces a new highway; the President issues an executive order; the mayor announces a new city plan.

The real "dirt" on what's going on in the government often comes from anonymous informants or whistleblowers. Laws have been passed to assure that bureaucratic whistleblowers are protected from recrimination, but the bureaucracy almost always persecutes them into leaving, or filing suit and leaving. The safest way to broadcast information is still the leak to a reporter.

At the national level, one of the problems is that reporters don't like to cover government agencies. Washington writer Stephen Hess noted a few years back that reporters in that city "resist assignments they think are dull" (the departments of agriculture, commerce, treasury, and the regulatory agencies). He implies that the reporters seem easily bored, especially TV reporters, and that government agencies seem to repel reporters. Reporters, he observed, tend to identify with the political types and agencies' heads who come and go every few years, not with the permanent government of civil servants. "By not connecting with the permanent government, reporters reinforce the lack of historical memory in news gathering," he noted.[8]

In the last few years, this seems to have changed somewhat at the national level. Part of the change comes from the fact that interest groups— both environmental and prodevelopment—have zeroed in on the workings of government agencies such as Environmental Protection Agency (EPA) and the Department of Interior, forcing the media to take more interest. There has also been more coverage of the Department of Health and Human Services and the Food and Drug Administration as issues such as national health care, AIDS, silicone breast implants, prescription medicines, diet, and drug abuse have become more of a concern in society.

Agency heads, following administration policy, often find themselves wearing the "Emperor's new clothes" in front of "60 Minutes" cameras as they attempt to explain away actions that lack credibility and may even be illegal. At the same time, as public servants, they are finding that in these days of constant communication, it's hard to hide.

Government agencies at the regional, state, and local levels have also become more media-conscious in recent years. Because more and more government managers have to deal with the public at meetings and are likely to have to talk with reporters, media- and community-relations training has become more prevalent.

The public-information policy at government offices usually falls into one of three modes: (1) all calls are handled by the public relations office; (2) only the agency head speaks to the media; and (3) any agency official may speak to the media on the record. The last and most enlightened policy is the least common. The chief counsel for EPA's Atlanta office, John Barker, makes sure his attorneys are not only able and ready to communicate with the media, but he also has a written policy absolving them if a media interview comes out negative. Even the most experienced spokespeople make flubs every day. The action by Mr. Barker overcame a major cultural problem of government people: a natural fear of being wronged by the media.

The Reagan years brought sophisticated public-issue management communications to the fore. The era of Republican White House Communication gurus like Michael Deaver, James Baker, Robert Teeter, Roger Ailes, and Lee Attwater introduced the era of the "spin doctor" who could take a negative event and cast it in a positive light, or vice versa. A spin doctor gets the media to focus on his client or position. Can this result in a distortion of the truth? John Scanlon of Daniel J. Edleman Worldwide responds, "Truth is not necessarily a solid. It can be a liquid."[9] Could someone make a silk purse into a sow's ear? Only if the audience would buy it, and for a long run, there was a willing audience. The 1990s have seen an ebb in this form of aggressive, sometimes very hostile public relations, but it, like the ghost of Willie Horton, lives on.

## HIGH-PROFILE TIMES FOR NONPROFITS

If there is an area where communication is king, it's in the nonprofit sector. The very reason for an association is to listen to members, to communicate their positions and represent them, and to provide feedback.

The American Society of Association Executives alone has 20,000 members representing 9,000 associations that speak for 215 million people. That's a healthy fraction of the U.S. population. Overall, there are 100,000 associations in the United States. The number of associations has nearly doubled in the past decade and a half.[10]

Associations are usually seen by the media as more credible than their members because they are generally seen as less self-serving. This gives the association the ability to defend and represent their members in a way that individual members cannot or may not want to. Associations promote their members with the media, deal with difficult issues that members might not want to be visible on, and track data that the media need.

Associations find themselves commenting on issues today ranging from hot stories in the news, like the Clarence Thomas-Anita Hill controversy, to proposed health-care legislation, to the effects of fad diets.

## MARKETING IN THE NONPROFIT SECTOR

In the 1980s, we witnessed the coming of age for management in the nonprofit sector. Cutbacks in government grants were partially responsible for a new bottom-line orientation. Also responsible was the cult status of being an M.B.A. in this period. During this time, many young, affluent managers began to take active roles in the arts and charities, joining boards and helping with fundraising. In the education area, universities faced with rising costs and dwindling enrollments moved aggressively to incorporate marketing into their communication activities. Nonprofit hospitals, riding a wave of belief that better business management would help them deal with government cost controls, began aggressively marketing new services such as backache centers, sports medicine, birthing programs, and the like. Arts organizations such as symphonies, theaters, and prominent museums were also smitten with the marketing craze.

Nonprofit groups decided it was time to go beyond publicity and public service and focus on delivering a product or service from a comprehensive marketing perspective that aimed to influence the behavior of their consumers. Organizations have realized that high visibility obtained through effective public relations must be generated through direct-mail solicitations, fund-raising campaigns, and other marketing efforts.

Through focusing communications efforts into marketing, the nonprofit organization reaches a wide range of constituencies: members, fundraising sources, clients, boards of directors, and more. Also, a nonprofit group usually relies on a number of different funding sources, and must target marketing efforts in many directions. One of marketing's greatest strengths is its ability to organize communication activities into a strategy that affects behavior.

More than ever, the accent is on identifying these key publics, establishing targets for each group, and developing the strategies based on effective consumer research. For example, one of the popular marketing umbrellas for nonprofits has been "belonging." One "belongs" to the symphony or art center or aquarium "family" and receives special privileges: first place in line at a new exhibit, or an opportunity to rub shoulders with the visiting dance company, or an invitation to members' night at the zoo. Exclusivity, membership, and belonging can be purchased for a $50-a-year donation.

Colleges have used similar approaches. At the University of Notre Dame, you can belong to the Sorin Club for $1,000 a year and rub elbows with the university's president. For $50 a year, you can be in the lottery for football tickets. Invitations are sent out for annual alumni days, when professors lecture on lighter subjects in business and the arts. Colleges give honorary degrees to public figures, and the old grads bask in the afterglow.

Public-interest and cause activists are also more sensitive to their constituencies. High-profile organizations like Greenpeace, the National Rifle Association, and the American Civil Liberties Union try to stir things up in the media in order to gain high visibility to maintain their organization's credibility and garner financial support from their constituencies. This can mean challenges in the courts, the legislature, and the bureaucracy to showcase the group's efforts to members. Good press coverage of a crusader leading a charge is a sure sign to contributors that things are happening.

Today, nonprofit organizations are well aware that public relations without marketing is not very effective. In one Illinois community a number of years ago, great publicity attended the highly anticipated opening of a new theater group. Heavy advance sales predicted a bright future for the group. Unfortunately, the first play was too highbrow for the audience and the theater group folded after the first season. Good public relations, but poor marketing. Of course, the argument is made that we're dealing with art and that there's no accounting for taste. But the fact is that art needs an audience.

One of the great marketing innovations in the arts in the last 20 years was the recognition that the sale of season subscriptions could provide the solid footing an arts organization needs. The foremost promoter of this approach was Danny Newman of Chicago's Lyric Opera Company.

## NONPROFIT EXAMPLES

An example of effective nonprofit sector marketing is the situation involving restoration of the Statue of Liberty. The Statue of Liberty-Ellis Island Foundation, having raised over $310 million to honor and restore the Statue of Liberty, still needed an additional $5 million to complete restoration of Ellis Island. and to develop a permanent museum. Based on research, the organization found that would-be givers with family ties to Ellis Island had felt left out of the original project, which had a lot of commercial involvement. So, an Immigrant Wall of Honor was conceived, which for $100, would list the name of a donor or his forebear in a permanent exhibit. Targeted audiences included ethnic and mature groups, history publications, and inflights. A tour around the United States involved presentations to local mayors honoring their own heritage. The final outcome was collection of $25 million—five times the goal.

Baltimore's Catholic schools also demonstrated effective marketing. The schools, facing a 20-percent decline in enrollment, inaugurated a marketing communications program. A high-visibility campaign was developed that emphasized academic excellence, value-centered teaching, and discipline, based on positive attributes identified in the preliminary research. The campaign included a massive second-hand book collection, encouraging media coverage, and, most importantly, teaching local principals how to do their own neighborhood marketing. Results showed that the 20-percent decline was reduced to just one percent.[11]

## BASIC GOVERNMENT AND NONPROFIT COMMUNICATIONS

As always, the manager attempting to launch or evaluate a communications program in the government or nonprofit sector has concerns about the cost of staffing such an operation. Communications programs in all sectors are being maintained at minimal levels. New technologies and use of outside services are increasingly taking on the workload.

Here are some cost-effective communications tools for today's small public/nonprofit communications department.

### The Basic Program

In almost every office, the basic communication and marketing tools are already in place:

1. Telephone with voice mail—voice mail allows communications on a time-shifted basis. The important thing is to return the calls promptly. An answering machine is the minimum requirement.

2. Mailing list—computer programs abound to help establish a mailing list for members. A data base that will have many more uses in the future is necessary. You can start small with a list of members, then add potential members, media contacts, influentials, friendly people in the public arena, and affiliated organizations.

3. Fax—a status icon you may not need but today you've got to have.

4. Pamphlet—Use a simple three-fold that fits in a number 10 envelope and explains why your organization exists. Some questions and answers about the organization are also valuable.

5. Speech—All organizations should have a canned 10-minute speech on their mission that anyone can give.

6. Graphic symbol—It may not be from a high-end New York design firm, but your organization needs a mark that graphically represents it.

7. Newsletter—Desktop publishing has made doing newsletters easy. Clip art, preprinted formats, and even canned articles are available to get you launched.

### Slide Show/Video

An organization that needs to expand its outreach effort or has a somewhat difficult-to-describe program should develop a slide show for informational purposes. Photos should be professionally shot, and running time should be under 20 minutes. The best format is to read it live as you are showing the slides, to make the presentation more personal. With new video technologies like Hi-8, you also can produce a video about your organization, quickly and inexpensively.

### Toll-Free Hotlines

The cost of "800" numbers has dropped substantially and gives your members a feeling that they're getting something for their money. The real cost to you is staffing that hotline. It is important to have a real person on the other end who can help members when they call.

### Speakers Bureau

A major urban utility that was being attacked by consumer and environmental organizations on a regular basis decided that the way to get their message across was to use company volunteers to speak to community groups on a number of topics. This approach can be very effective. It provides a chance for a real person to represent the organization and be able to engage in give-and-take with the audience.

### Free Publicity

Many radio and television stations regularly run community service calendars that will announce your event or activity. Others will run public-service announcements of varying length. All you need to do is provide the copy. Newspapers also run community calendars, and it's quite possible to get them to give you publicity for various events. In addition, many radio and television programs try to book interest group spokespeople, especially in this day of cable TV. Many broadcast public affairs programs were ended when the Federal Communications Commission lifted its public-service programming requirements.

### Awards Program

Awards programs are an excellent vehicle for developing publicity and goodwill. Stage an annual awards program. In a brochure, to recognize people who support the goals of your organization, set out categories and rules for nomination. Encourage submissions that contain testimonial materials. Evaluate with a blue ribbon panel. Then, hold a luncheon, invite a prominent speaker or sports figures, and pass out awards. Try to get media coverage. This is a good project for organizations that are frequently involved in conflict-oriented activities, because it provides a chance for the group to show its more positive side. Reject paying celebrities for an appearance, however. It's unethical, or at least disingenuous.

### Press Support

A list of subject-matter experts available to the press from an organization can generate significant publicity over time. An occasional visit to the news desks also provides face-to-face contact that can pay off later.

### Hollywood

The issues your organization deals with may very well provide an excellent plot for today's news and news-driven dramatic and comedy TV series. Send your most flamboyant member to Hollywood to hang out with TV writers and sell them ideas. Much good information can be transmitted to the public via the arts—offbeat ventures like photo exhibits, dramatic radio programming, and touring musical companies carrying a message offer an excellent message platform.

## ENDNOTES

1. David Osborne, "Government That Means Business," *New York Times Magazine*, March 1, 1992, p. 20.
2. *Ibid.*

3. Thaddeus H. Spratlen, "Government Goods and Services: Characteristics and Concepts for Marketing Analysis," in Michael P. Mokwa and Stephen E. Pennut (eds.):; *Government Marketing* (New York, Proeger, 1981), pp. 36–51.

4. "Introducing the Shore Line East Commuter Rail Service," *1001 Silver Anvil Winners Index and Summaries* (New York: Public Relations Society of America), pp. 51–52.

5. James W. Montore, "A Bi-State Regional Approach to Marketing," *Economic Development Review*, 7, no. 3 (Summer 1989), pp. 20–23.

6. Frank M. Corrado, *Media for Managers* (New Jersey: Prentice-Hall, 1984), pp. 189–90.

7. *Ibid.*, p. 190–91.

8. Stephen Hess, *The Washington Reporters* (Washington, D.C.: Brookings Institution, 1981), p. 126.

9. John Scanlon, interview by Adam Smith, February 15, 1991, on "Power and Persuasion: How PR Shapes the News," "Adam Smith's Money World," WNET-TV, New York.

10. Helen Frank Bensimon and Patricia A. Walker, "Associations Gain Prestige and Visibility by Serving as Expert Resources for Media," *Public Relations Journal*, February 1992, pp. 14–16.

11. "The Ellis Island Immigration Museum," pp. 29–30; and "Catholic Schools: A Valuable Education. An Education in Values," *1001 Silver Anvil Winners Index and Summaries*, pp. 59–60.

## Appendix B

# Measuring Communications Value

With the hard-nosed management realities of the future, all communication activities will have to show—by the numbers—that they can provide a return on investment, and that they can create value in three areas: (1) increasing the productivity of employees, (2) positioning the organization effectively with external constituencies, and (3) selling products or services.

Measuring success in these areas will not be an easy task, especially in light of the historical lack of interest by communicators in measurement and evaluation. Communications people have traditionally focused on goal-oriented activities, generating materials and disseminating them, with little evaluation or feedback beyond number of stories run or total column inches of coverage.

For managers trying to work with communications professionals, this has been a source of conflict. Public relations people are often viewed as (and view themselves as) creative, intuitive, free spirits who can work some sort of black magic in handling internal and external corporate audiences, providing solutions that cannot be equated to formulas and numbers. Though many colleagues may not agree, the author believes there is some validity to the intuitive approach.

There is a lot of successful right-brain activity in business—the entrepreneur with the timely idea, the salesperson who knows egos, the plant manager who sets the tone, the CEO who inspires employees by force of personality. Can these be reduced to formulas and numbers? No. Neither can great public relations ideas.

Nevertheless, a company needs to understand how the communication activities it engages in create value for the organization, and the only way to effectively establish this is to prove that the communications process can achieve greater productivity, an increase in sales, and a more positive public image for its environmental actions.

Managers *and* communicators today are both concerned about the efficacy of communication. The manager realizes that communication is becoming more important in the business environment. The communicator realizes that he or she must become more strategic or be replaced. Therefore, there is a mutual interest in measurement and evaluation. This does not mean that creativity should be minimized, but rather, it should be as supported as advertising is.

## PUBLIC RELATIONS RESEARCH AND PUBLIC RELATIONS

The questions have been long standing: How do you know what you do works? How do you move the needle? How do you justify your program at budget time? The answer is—use research.

There are four reasons why an organization should do communication research.

1. There may be high stakes riding on the outcome. Remember the public opinion sampling that drove the Tylenol crisis?
2. Multiple issues may be involved. There may be a reason beyond the obvious conclusions.
3. There's no single expert to go to for answers. In dealing with the behavior of people, one cannot easily predict outcomes.
4. There's a need to give a reason or justification for a communications decision.[1]

If a company spends $50,000 on a public-relations program to build goodwill in the community, how will it know if the program worked?

Since public relations deals with establishing a receptive public environment for the organization to operate in, communication activities should normally follow the classic planning process (Figure B-1), which includes defining a goal, establishing a plan or strategy to achieve that goal, implementing the plan, evaluating impact, and beginning the entire process over again.

## INFORMAL EVALUATION

The story is told about the CEO who is confronted by the public relations director and warned of a major problem. ''I don't see a problem. Nobody's

**FIGURE B-1**
*The Classic Planning Process*

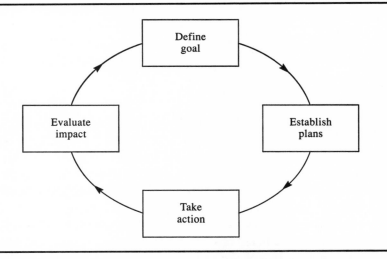

told me about that," says the CEO, bewildered. And he's right: nobody at *his* club, nobody in *his* circle of friends, or even in *his* neighborhood has seen the problem because his environment is so insulated. To evaluate, he needs to get out and look around.

There are a number of informal ways a manager can evaluate an organization's communication activities:

- Walkarounds—How do people address each other? What are the clues to status or job—dress, parking, eating areas? How do people get together—in closed offices, in the hall? What's on the bulletin boards? Does the suggestion box look used? Are there any motivators on the walls—signs, posters, and so forth? Do people seem busy and happy with their work?

- Lunch-room surveys—Informal discussions at the lunch table, the vending machine, in the restroom. What are people talking about? What are they worried about? What's the grapevine saying?

- Interviews/focus groups—Internally and externally, what are people's concerns when you get them together? How do people react when you bring up certain topics?

- Reading/viewing communications materials—Is the newsletter coming out on time? What kinds of stories is it telling—bowling scores or production reports? What do the press clippings look like?

- Stories people tell—Is there some pattern to what people are saying? Do the stories talk about successes or failures?
- Feedback channels—What's in the suggestion box? What's on the "800" line? What is the sales/field force reporting?

## FORMAL MEASUREMENT

Many times in public relations, a goal is stated in terms of the effort and not the results: "Our goal is to warn the public about the dangers of high fat diets"; or "Our goal is to tell the story of the Widget's return to the marketplace." The problem here is that there is nothing measurable.

The first concern is measuring the *impact* of the communications efforts. A close parallel exists here between measuring communications and performance appraisal. In a performance appraisal program, measurable objectives are established for the employee at the beginning of the rating period. For example, "LTAs (lost time due to accidents) will be reduced by 5 percent during the evaluation period." "Customer complaints will decrease to less than three per month," and so on. This kind of specificity is used, as opposed to more general statements, such as, "Will make an effort to reduce LTAs." In communications, the classic goals talk in terms of outputs, not impacts. The problem can be seen in the following classic communications measurements:

1. *Readership surveys*, which only measure the fact that people were attracted to an article. They do not measure whether that article influenced their actions.

2. *Content analysis*, which measures whether communication materials match the outcome expectations spelled out in the objectives.

3. *Readability Indexes*, which can tell you whether your material is understandable for your targeted audience.

4. *Tracking*, which evaluates print or video clips by recording placement, distribution, column inches, and other measures such as equivalent cost of buying similar space. These only tell you where the information is going, not whether it is having an impact.

**FIGURE B–2**
*Hierarchy of Measurement Techniques*

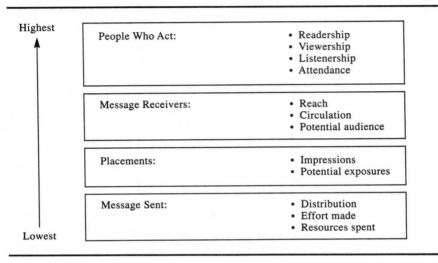

5. *Audience*, which is discovered by research. Research distinguishes among the audience that you can potentially reach, the audience you actually reached, and your target audience.

These techniques work very well in helping make adjustments to an ongoing program, but are not useful for measuring the impact of a program.

Figure B–2 demonstrates that there is a hierarchy to traditional measurement techniques. The goal is measurement of behavior change as a result of communication.[2]

In measuring the impact of communication, effectiveness has been generally evaluated based on communication activities—delivering a message via the media to the public. This approach is characteristic of *press agentry/ publicity activities* and *public-information programs*.[3] With press agentry and publicity, which include activities like product promotion, movies, and sports, we evaluate success by counting the attendees. How many people showed up? How many articles did we get? Beyond this, there is no evaluation. An estimated 15 percent of organizations run their communications this way.

With a public-information approach, which is also a one-way process, there is also little evaluation, except for occasional readership or readabil-

**TABLE B–1**
*Four Communication Models*

| 15% | 50% | 20% | 15% |
|---|---|---|---|
| Press | Public | Feedback | Dialogue |
| Agent | Information | | |
| No feedback | Little feedback | Asymmetrical | Symmetrical |

ity studies. It's been estimated that about half of all public relations is practiced in this manner, mostly in government, nonprofit organizations, and some businesses. In both public information and press agentry, communication is one way. There is no built-in feedback.

A third approach involves using some type of feedback to evaluate the effectiveness of the publicity or public information. It is estimated that about 20 percent of communication programs follow this approach. The research measures attitudes before and after the campaign. This approach is called *asymmetric* and is often used by businesses and agencies involved in marketing and public affairs work.

The fourth model, symmetrical, involves two-way communication and is characteristic of mostly regulated business and agencies, such as hospitals or an organization attempting to site a landfill. An estimated 15 percent of communication programs are conducted in this manner. Table B–1 shows different communications models and what percentage they represent of communication programs and evaluation methods utilized.[4]

The trend today is away from the traditional measurement techniques and more towards a "cybernetic" approach (towards the right of the scale in Table B–1), as public relations take on a more prominent role in marketing, and budgets increase.

The International Association of Business Communicators (IABC) has identified *Symmetrical* communications as their model for the 1990s because it is based on two-way communication with targeted audiences. The model is also *cybernetic* and allows modification by both message sender and receiver. Evaluation is based in behavioral science rather than in media relations. IABC believes that this model will bring the communicator to a higher, more strategic level in decision making because with the symmetrical style, changes in behavior occur both within the organization and with the target.[5]

With this approach, IABC researchers believe that public relations can be defined in a way that will move the profession more towards behavioral science. The emphasis will be on communicating with targeted publics more than with the media.

## MEASUREMENTS AND EVALUATION

A number of fields, including marketing and advertising, provide classic research models—mass communications, persuasion, and organizational communication, to name a few. With any approach, an important consideration is determining whether the message has moved the receiver *to take the desired action*.

Communications for Management's research on *internal communications*, under the direction of consultant Robert Nadeau[6], started with the assumption that linking communication efforts to the goals of the organization is a foremost concern today for communicators. The key issues behind those concerns are these: How does communication create value for an organization? and How can this value be measured? The need for this approach comes from today's organizational realities—that companies exist to create value, and value is determined by economic performance in the marketplace. By increasing the amount of goal-oriented action by its people, an organization will improve its economic performance.

So, value is created from the effective allocation of resources—including people—which results in economic performance (creation of value) designed to achieve corporate goals. (See Figure B–3.)

Effective formal and informal communication motivates people (stakeholders) to take goal-oriented actions that will produce value, as seen in Figure B–4.

Characteristics of this communication-centered approach are that it:

- Promotes understanding and commitment.
- Seeks feedback and participation.
- Provides motivation.
- Creates a basis for action.
- Monitors progress towards accomplishment of organizational goals.

The role of communication here is to move people towards goal-oriented action, not just compliance or passive acceptance of the information.

**FIGURE B–3**
*The Creation of Value*

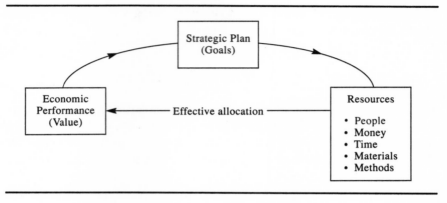

**FIGURE B–4**
*Creating Value with Communication*

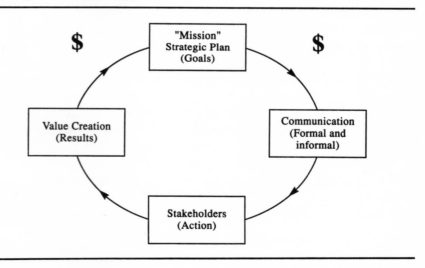

The objective is to be able to measure some behavioral change, or, at a minimum, movement on the scale shown here in Figure B–5.

Here are the definitions of terms used in Figure B–5.

- Aware—have general awareness of the issue.
- Inform—up-to-date on issues involved.

**FIGURE B–5**
*Measuring the Value of Communication*

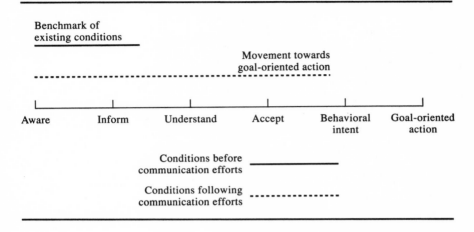

- Understand—have full knowledge of the issue and implications.
- Accept—mentally accept the validity of the issue.
- Intent—have decided to take action, but have not yet carried it out.
- Goal-oriented action—take specific action requested.

This approach, using standard research techniques, provides data that enable management to:

1. Establish a benchmark of existing conditions.
2. Identify the information needs of various stakeholder groups in relation to the goals of the organization.
3. Identify effective channels and media.
4. Align communication policies and practices to the goals of the organization.
5. Develop a long-range communication strategy.
6. Identify forces and factors that could impede successful accomplishment of organizational goals.
7. Measure the relationship between communication efforts and economic performance.

**FIGURE B–6** *Communications Model Modified to Show Behavior Change Impact on Value Creation*

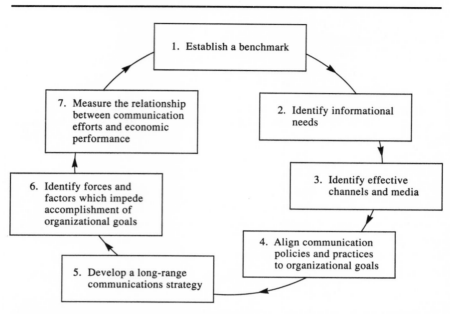

The full process is described graphically in Figure B–6 above. This adaptation of the classic communications model is unique because it includes measurement of communication's efforts.

## QUANTITATIVE VERSUS QUALITATIVE RESEARCH

As communicators take their first steps towards research, they have tended to lean towards qualitative over quantitative. The most popular qualitative techniques include interviews and focus groups. Focus groups of 6 to 12 people can be organized and conducted relatively quickly over a one-to-three-hour period. In that length of time, you can identify an audience, test a message, and confirm the direction you're going. In addition, focus groups are relatively inexpensive. A company seeking to embark on a community relations program in a community might bring in influential people for focus groups to test the reaction to its proposed program.

Researchers generally tend to look down their noses at this technique unless it is tied to an actual survey because it lacks the scientific validity that formal survey research provides.

Another qualitative technique, the in-depth interview, provides an open-ended interview, in which the interviewee is given a subject and then encouraged to expand on it in his or her own terms. This kind of research is valuable early in the process to evaluate the kind of climate or environment that the research will be conducted in.

The normal quantitative research tool is the survey. Questionnaires are generally more expensive to develop, test, and administer. They range from the more elaborate face-to-face interview to a short, down-and-dirty telephone interview. Questionnaires may be passed out at the office or plant for the employee to fill out, or mailed tp the employee to be done at home. The design and administration of questionnaires should be conducted by professional researchers, usually outside contractors.

*Indirect* causes of problems can also be discovered through survey research. For example, concern about famine and hunger in the world might be the reason why people in a community are willing to allow a company to conduct genetic tests, rather than giving any arguments over the safety of testing.[7]

## EVALUATING INTERNAL COMMUNICATIONS

The classic tools for diagnoses of communications problems in organizations are (1) the attitude survey, (2) the communication survey, and (3) the communication audit. CM believes that the value creation model should be the overarching evaluation method for any of these internal communication diagnostics.

An employee attitude survey measures a wide range of subjects including climate, security, job satisfaction, opportunity communication, management, compensation, and benefits.

A communication survey measures:

- Communication philosophy.
- Topics important to employees.
- Whether employees feel sufficiently informed.
- What their preferred sources of information are.
- How high readership levels for publications are.

- Rating of communications for credibility and usefulness.
- Managers' communication skills.
- Awareness by employees of the company's mission/vision/values, to name some.

One of the major issues in communication surveys or employee attitude surveys is what to do with the data once you've got it. These surveys, which are sometimes evaluated against national norms, provide both direct and normative information to management. For example, an electric utility may learn that only 43 percent of its managers feel that they get enough information from upper management to do their job adequately. While this number may appear to be a cause for concern, when compared with other electric utilities from across the country, the number may be considered average and therefore not of special concern. In the CM value creation model, however, the real issue is how to measure employee movement towards achievement of corporate goals. We feel this information is more relevant to the needs of management.

A communication audit looks at:

- Both formal and informal communications channels.
- Upward and downward flow of information.
- Lateral communication.
- Employee preferences for communication.

Audits model how the communication process works in the organization, based on the stated goals, resources committed, and perceptions of the employees. An audit can determine (1) how credible management is, (2) employee attitudes and company knowledge, (3) effectiveness of feedback programs, (4) impact of corporate media, and (5) effectiveness of supervisory communications.[8]

Techniques used in communication audits include:

- *Focus groups* are small groups of people representing various demographic cuts of employee groups. Focus groups provide qualitative information, which includes not only their opinions, but the context for those opinions.
- *Management climate assessment* is generally a series of interviews with top management and key unit managers to determine the culture and values of the organization in relation to communication. Also used to identify the effects of individual personalities and define the content of jobs and roles.

- *Content evaluation of published material* looks at the subject matter of memos, policies, forms, newsletters, the paper that a corporation runs on to determine what is important, based on what is written down and kept.
- *Surveys* provide a means to let everyone in the organization get involved in the audit process. Surveys allow people to participate anonymously. Data is quantitative.
- *Network analysis* looks at the interaction between people in an organization to determine or map such things as communication nodes or bottlenecks. The theory is that the more people interact, the more successful the organization is.[9]

## COMMUNICATIONS RESEARCH AND CHANGE

One of the real problems with research is that sometimes it tells you what you don't want to hear—that the community is set against your proposed waste site and is not likely to change; that management is hopelessly out of touch with its employees; that there is no market for your product.

Those people who stand to lose the most will try to find ways to discredit the research. So, it's important to set up a process for getting past this problem:

1. Provide feedback that makes sense.
2. Get commitment to take action before doing the research.
3. Relate actions to research—tell people that their input helped.
4. Measure how actions worked—find out if what you did worked.[10]

The level of reaction to research can range from full implementation to full rejection, with the worst outcome probably being a decision to do nothing.

Often, research is used for symbolic purposes—whitewashing a failure, torpedoing a program, or postponing or delaying a project. The best use of communication research is to help in choosing among possible alternatives during the design of communications and then making organizational changes that respond to feedback.

The movement towards evaluation can only help people in the communications field. It's a maturing step, one that has become necessary because of a general recognition of the increasing importance of improving human resource performance and competing successfully in the new work market-place.

## ENDNOTES

1. Glenn M. Broom and David M. Dozier, *Using Research in Public Relations* (Englewood Cliffs, New Jersey: Prentice Hall, 1990), p. 51.
2. *Ibid.*, p. 70.
3. The following is a description of the Grunig-Hunt model of public relations, adapted from Carolyn Garrett Cline, Ph.D., *Evaluation and Measurement in Public Relations and Organizational Communication: A Literature Review*, 1984, IABC Foundation research report, pp. 71–76.
4. *Ibid.*
5. Judith Carrington, "Establishing a More Strategic Role in PR Practice: Why, How, and When?" *IABC Communication World*, February 1992, pp. 17–20.
6. Robert Nadeau, Linking Communication to the Goals of the Organization, Chicago, Communications for Management, Inc. International White Paper, 1992.
7. Broom and Dozier, "Using Research in Public Relations," pp. 261–62.
8. Seymour Hamilton, *A Communication Audit Handbook, Helping Organizations Communicate* (London: Longman, 1987), pp. 3–5.
9. *Ibid.*, pp. 57–67.
10. Broom and Dozier, "Using Research in Public Relations," p. 295.

# Index

**A**

Account executive communications,
support model, 35
Adolph Coors, 105
Ailes, Roger, 182
Akers, John F., 16
Allstate Insurance, 174
Alyesaka Pipeline Company, 160,
172
AMC Corp., 173
American Civil Liberties Union, 184
American Enterprise Institute, 127
Amerman, John, 22
Anderson, Warren M., 163
Annual report, 129
Anthony M. Franco, Inc., 94
Arctic National Wildlife Refuge, 12
Arm & Hammer, 84
AT&T, 3, 42, 59, 157, 160
Atwater, Lee, 182
Audience, 195
Audio-visual technology, changes in, 36–
37
Authoritarian organization
climate of, 40
model, 43–44

**B**

Baker, James, 182
Baker, Russell, 3
Barker, John, 182
*Barron's*, 142
Beef Industry Council, 93

Behavior change model, 91
Benchmarking, 57–58
Benefits communication, 75–76
Benefits communication plan
developing, 76–77
tools of, 77–78
Bernays, Edward L., 28
Bill of Rights, 134, 138, 154
Body Shop, The, 83, 103
Boeing Aircraft, 118
Booz Allen & Hamilton, 99
Brennan, Edward A., 16
British Air, 3, 13
Brochures, 22–23
Burke, James, 12, 158
Burson-Marstellar, 37, 91
Bush, George, 20, 98, 140
Business communications; *see also*
Financial communications
requirements of, 134
Business-media-hostility theories, 136
*Business Week*, 97

**C**

Cable News Network (CNN), 1, 137–38,
156
CAER; *see* Community Awareness and
Emergency Response
Campbell, 83, 84
National Soup Month, 83
Carter, Jimmy, 158
Caterpillar, 54
CBS, 154
"CBS Evening News," 138

CEO and communications
  importance of, 12–14
  showing CEO disease, 15
  ways to avoid, 15–16
CERCLA; *see* Comprehensive
  Environmental Resource
  Conservation and Liability Act
Champion International, 11
Chemical Manufacturers Association, 93,
  160
Chicago Board of Trade emissions
  futures, 100
Chrysler, 11, 151
  Jefferson Avenue North plant, 64
Clean Air Act, 14, 100
Coca Cola 31
  Diet Coke, 83, 84
Communicating vision, 20–22
Communication
  impact on CEO, 9–16, 19
  impact on management, 5
  role of, 5, 7
Communication in government, 181–83
  external, 181
  internal, 181
Communication materials, development
  of, 68
Communication plan
  key elements, 76
  tools, 77–78
Communications
  evolving responsibilities of, 29–30
  imperatives of, 4–5
  organizational strategy, 33
  organizing and staffing, 31–32
  professional qualifications of, 28–29
  strategic model, 32
Communications evaluation model, 23
Communications executive,
  responsibilities of, 31–32
Communications firms, 37
Communications for Management, Inc.,
  International, 51
Communications research
  qualitative techniques, 200–201
  quantitative techniques, 201

Communications strategy, 27
Communications strategy, for cutting
  costs, 78
Communication technology, 22–23, 60
Communication tools, 77
Communication variance, 91
Community Awareness and Emergency
  Response (CAER), 160
Community relations, 37
Compaq, 3
Compensation communications, 72–75
  communications goals, 73
  identifying targets and needs, 73–74
  selecting media, 74
  subject goals, 73
  timing and training, 75
Comprehensive Environmental Resource
  Conservation and Liability Act
  (CERCLA), 101
Conference Board, The, 49, 50, 54, 61,
  104, 122, 127
Confrontational crises, basic rules of,
  174
Congress General Accounting Office
  studies, 180
Connecticut Department of
  Transportation, 179
Consumer relations, 130–31
*Consumer Reports,* 87
Content analysis, 194
Content evaluation, 203
Corporate communications
  costs of 34, 36
  financing, 34
  function of, 94
  importance of, 49
  internal, 50
  new initiatives, 59
  statistics, 49
Corporate communications director, role
  of, 19–20
Corporate communications
  responsibilities, 27–28
Corporate environmental
  communications, improving, 101–2,
  114

Corporate issues, 120
Corporate publications, crucial topics of, 47–48
Corporate public relations, 93
Council on Economic Priorities, 93–94
Credibility, 10
Crisis
anticipation of, 160
definition of, 167
reaction to, 160
Crisis communication, 27, 119
Crisis simulation exercise, 170
Crisis team
responsibilities of, 169
three groups of, 166
Cross-impact analysis, 122
"A Current Affair," 138, 143
Customer relations; see Consumer relations


**D**

Daniel J. Edleman Worldwide, 182
Dealing with media; see also Reaching media
local versus national, 144–45
preparation, 144
Deaver, Michael, 182
Delphi study, 170
Deming, Crosby, Juran, 41
Denton, Harold, 158
Department of Interior, 182
Department of Health and Human Services, 182
DePree, Max, 19
Developing media relations, 141–43
policy considerations, 141
Digital Equipment, 22
Direct marketing, 85
Dow Jones, 129
Downsizing impacts, negative, 69
Drexel Burnham Lambert, 17, 18, 157
Drucker, Peter, 39
DuPont, 12

**E**

E-mail, 22
Emergency Planning and Right-to-Know Act of 1986, 104
Employee communications planning
establishing objectives, 57
information needs, 56
suggestions for improvement, 57–59
Employee participation in decision making, 43
Employee performance, motivations for, 48
Employee suggestion program, 19, 48; see also Empowering
Empowering, 19
"Entertainment Tonight," 143
Environmental Defense Fund, 102
Environmental efforts, proactive, 101
Environmental program, proactive, 100-101
Environmental Protection Agency (EPA), 182
Evaluating internal communications, 201–3
Expert opinion, 171
Exxon, 5, 12
Valdez disaster, 5, 99, 133, 160, 163, 172

**F**

Federal Emergency Management Agency, 169
Federal Trade Commission, 103
Financial communications, 129–30; see also Business communications
annual report, 129
disclosure requirements of, 129
role of, 129
Financial investor relations, 27
Firestone, 29, 87
500 radial tire, 29
Flacks, 118
Focus groups, 202
Food and Drug Administration, 182

*Forbes,* 144
Ford, 29
Fortune 500, 142
  companies, 32, 65, 99
Foster and Crosby, 49
Freedom of Information Act, 133
Freeman, Audrey, 54
Fulfilling responsibilities, for supervisors
  and management, 53–54


**G**

General Electric (GE), 3, 13, 32, 42
General Motors Corp. (GM), 4, 11, 17,
  40, 42
*Getting to Yes* (Fisher and Ury), 113,
  174
"Good Morning, America," 89
Government relations, 27
Grapevine, 43
Green Cross, 103
Green issues, impact on business, 99–
  100
Green marketing, 5
  public involvement, 107–9
  standards, 102–4
Greenpeace, 174, 184
Green Seal mark, 103
Gutfreund, John, 134


**H**

Haig, Alexander, 160
Harrison, E. Bruce, 99
Havel, Vaclav, 141
Hay Group, 49
  studies, 10
Hay Management, 81
Helping survivors, nine-step process, 70–
  71
Herman Miller, Inc., 19
Hess, Stephen, 181
High concept news, 139
Hill & Knowlton, 37, 172
Honda Motors, 93

Horton, James, 172
Human resources
  initiatives, 64
  organizational strategy, 67
  special communications problems,
    68–76
  traditional activities, 65
Human resource strategy, 65
Hyde, Richard, 172


**I**

"I Witness," 19
Iacocca, Lee, 11, 151
*In Search of Excellence* (Peters and
  Waterman), 10
"Inside Edition," 138, 143
Interest group liaison, 27
International Association of Business
  Communicators (IABC), 28, 196
  certification, 28
International Business Machines Corp.
  (IBM), 4, 16, 17, 22, 31, 55
  *Speak Up!* program, 55
International intelligence, 128
Intuitive forecasting, 122
Investor relations; *see* Financial
  communications
Irvine, Robert B., 172
Issue life cycle, 123
Issues management, 119–28
  categories of, 120
  definition of, 119
  developing problems, 121–28
  identifying issues, 122
  impact of, 121
  process, 120


**J**

Johns Manville Corporation, 15–16,
  22
Johnson & Johnson, 12
  Tylenol case, 84, 156–59
Johnson, Robert Woods, 159

# K

Kerry, Bob, 152
King, Larry, 1
Kirban, Lloyd, 91
Koch, Ed, 105
Kosobud, Bob, 81
Kotler, Philip, 91
Kraft, 22

# L

Leadership
  challenges, 10
  needs, 9–10
Lesly, Philip, 7, 92
Levi Strauss & Co., 77, 171
  on-line interactive visual employee
    resource (OLIVER), 77
Lobbying, 125
Loblaw Co., 100
Lorrilard, 154
*Los Angeles Times* 137
Lou Harris poll, 10–11

# M

Mahoney, Richard J., 97
Management climate assessment, 202
Managerial communications, 43–44
Managing crisis, 160–64
Managing employee communication
  internal communications, 50
  methods of, 50–52
  responsibilities of, 49
Maples, Marla, 141
Marketing communications, 83
  components of, 84
  types of, 85
Marketing government services, 178–81
  elements of, 180
Marketing public relations, 93
Marketing warfare, 85
Materiality, 129
Mattel, 22

McDonald's, 84, 87, 101
Measuring communications value
  characteristics of, 197
  formal evaluation, 194–97
  informal evaluation, 192–94
  terms of, 198–99
Measuring impact, 23–24
Medialink, 89
Message platform, 94
Metropolitan Edison, 158
Meyers, Gerald C., 173
Milken, Mike, 118
Miller, Russ, 44
Monitoring events, 122
Monsanto Co., 97
Moyers, Bill, 140–41

# N

Nadeau, Robert, 52, 197
Nader, Ralph, 124
National Association of Manufacturers,
  126, 127
National Institutes of Health, 179
National Rifle Association, 184
Natural Resources Defense Council, 102
Network analysis, 203
Newlin, Patricia, 92
Newman, Danny, 185
Newsletters, 22–23
*New York Times,* 144
*New York Times* v. *Sullivan,* 153
Niederquell, Michael O., 94
NIMBY; *see* Not in my backyard
Nonprofit communications, 186–88
Nonprofit marketing, 183–85
Normative forecasting, 122
Not in my backyard, 105

# O

Office of Management and Budget, 125
Ogilvy, David, 86
Ontario Hydro, 33–34
Operational issues, 120

"Oprah Winphrey," 121
Osborne, David, 178
Outside-in theory, 60

**P**

PAC; *see* Political action committee
Page, Arthur, 42
Participatory democracy, 108
Participatory management, 41
Paul, Jane, 2
Pay for performance, 54
Pay gap, 11
Performance communication
  communication components, 49–80
  levels of, 79
Perot, Ross, 1, 139
Phelps, Lew, 33
"Phil Donahue," 121
Philip Morris, 85
Philips Petroleum, 128
Planning for crisis, 164–73
  accident versus emergency, 164
  five basic steps, 165–70
  key public messages, 161–63
  suggestions, 172–73
Political action committee (PAC), 126–27
Pollution prevention, 100
Positioning, 85
Predicting crisis, 170–71
Pressure groups, 121
Preston Trucking, 22
Proctor & Gamble (P & G), 31, 101, 133, 134, 143
Profitability
  link with communication, 44
  management guidelines for, 44–47
  methods for improving, 45–47
Public information policy, 182
Public relations, 84
  corporate, 93
  introduction to, 94–95
  marketing of, 93
  measurement tools, 91–92
  nicknames of, 118

Public Relations—*continued*
  role of, 84
  use in marketing, 86–89
Public Relations Society of America (PRSA), 28
  certification, 28

**R**

Rawls, Lawrence, 12, 99
RCRA; *see* Resource Conservation and Recovery Act
Reaching media; *see also* Dealing with media
  channels, 147–49
  media traps, 150–51
  special problems, 153
  suggestions, 149–50
  types of interviews, 151–53
Reactibility indexes, 194
Readership surveys, 194
Reagan, Ronald, 125, 139–40
*Reinventing Government* (Osborne), 17
Relationship marketing, 85
Resource Conservation and Recovery Act (RCRA), 101
Reuters, 129
Right-to-Life Foundation, 174
Risk
  involuntary, 110
  voluntary, 110
Risk communication, 109–13
  outrage factors, 112
RJR Nabisco, 50
Robinson, Lake & Palmer, 118
Rockefeller, John D., 118
*Rolling Stone,* 141

**S**

Salomon Brothers, 17, 134
Sandman, Peter M., 111
SARA; *see* Superfund Amendments and Reauthorization Act
SARA Title III; *see* Emergency Planning and Right-to-Know Act of 1986

Scanlon, John, 182
Scenario building and modeling, 122
Scenario development, 171
Schlickman, J. Andrew, 114
Schwarzkopf, Norman, 16
Sears, Roebuck & Co., 3, 16, 157
SEC; *see* Securities and Exchange
  Commission
Securities and Exchange Commission,
  11, 129, 133
Selchow and Righter, Trivial Pursuit, 83,
  89
Shapiro, Irving, 12, 135
Shills, 118–19
*Shopping for a Better World* (Council on
  Economic Priorities), 94
Sidley & Austin, 114
Sierra Club, 102
Signal, Andrew, 11
Single overriding communications
  objectives, 149
Single-platform approach, 160–61
"60 Minutes," 87, 133, 182
  report on Alar, 87, 133
Social marketing, 85
Societal issues, 120
SOCO; *see* Single overriding
  communications objectives
Soundbite journalism, 138–39
Source Perrier, 87, 157
Southern California Edison, 33
Southwest Airlines, 11
Speechwriting, 56
Spin doctor, 119
Staffing structure, 30
Stahl, Leslee, 139–40
StarKist policy on dolphin-safe tuna
  fishing, 87
Statute of Liberty-Ellis Island
  Foundation, 185
Stempel, 11
Steuben Glass, 17
Stone Container Corporation, 60
Strategic corporate communication, 87
Strategic support, 27
Superfund, 101

Superfund Amendments and
  Reauthorization Act, 161
Superfund law, 101
Surveys, 203
Survivors, 68–72
Sustainable development, 97–98


**T**

Tactical support, 36
Teeter, Robert, 182
Tele/video conferencing, 22
Temple, Barker and Sloan, 14
Thoreau, Henry David, 1
3M, 17, 10
Three Mile Island, 157–59, 161
"Today," 89
Tom's of Maine, 103
Total quality management, 80
Towers Perrin, 49
Toyota, 19
TPF&C, 44
TQM; *see* Total quality management
Tracking, 194
Trade association, 127
Trend extrapolation, 122, 171
Turner, Ted, 2, 138


**U**

U.S. Chamber of Commerce, 126, 127
Umbrella groups, 127
Underwriters Laboratory (UL), 104
  Green Seal mark, 104
Union Carbide, 163, 165
United Airlines, 164
United Services Automobile Association,
  118
Upward communications, 45, 55–56
*USA Today*, 4


**V**

Value creation model, 58
  suggestions for improvement, 57–59

Video, 22
Video news releases, 88
VNR; *see* Video news releases
Voice mail, 22

**W-X**

*Wall Street Journal, The,* 133, 144, 154
Wallace, Mike, 144
Wannamaker, John, 90
Warhol, Andy, 3
Warner, John, 2

*Washington Post,* 154
Weidenbaum, Murray, 125
Welch, Jack, 4
Westinghouse, George, 118
Westinghouse company, 32, 57
Weyerhauser Company study, 44–47
William M. Mercer company, 49
Withholding information, reasons for, 43
Workers compensation costs, strategy for
    cutting, 78
Wyatt Co., 42, 49
Xerox, 3, 13